Ian McEwan

IAN McEWAN

Ian McEwan

Kiernan Ryan

Northcote House

in association with
The British Council

© Copyright 1994 by Kiernan Ryan

First published in 1994 by Northcote House Publishers Ltd, Plymbridge House,
Estover Road, Plymouth PL6 7PZ, United Kingdom.
Tel: (0752) 735251. Fax: (0752) 695699.

British Library Cataloguing-in-Publication Data
A catalogue record for this book is available from the British Library

ISBN 0 7463 0742 X

Typeset by PDQ Typesetting, Stoke-on-Trent
Printed and bound in the United Kingdom by BPC Wheatons Ltd, Exeter

Contents

Acknowledgements

The author and the publishers are grateful to Ian McEwan and Jonathan Cape Ltd for permission to quote from the works of Ian McEwan, with the exception of *The Ploughman's Lunch*, for which thanks are due to Ian McEwan and Methuen, London.

Biographical Outline

1948	Ian Russell McEwan born 21 June in Aldershot, Hampshire, the son of a soldier in the British army.
1951–9	Army childhood abroad, chiefly Singapore and Tripoli.
1959–66	Attended state boarding-school at Woolverstone Hall, Suffolk.
1967–70	Read English and French at University of Sussex.
1970–1	Studied modern fiction and creative writing at University of East Anglia.
1972	Trip to Afghanistan and North-West Frontier Province.
1975	Somerset Maugham Award for *First Love, Last Rites*.
1976	Visit to USA.
1978	*In Between the Sheets* and *The Cement Garden*.
1980	*The Imitation Game*.
1981	*The Comfort of Strangers* nominated for Booker Prize.
1982	Married Penny Allen.
1983	Birth of son, William. *Or Shall We Die?* performed. *The Ploughman's Lunch*: Evening Standard Award for Best Screenplay.
1984	Fellowship of the Royal Society of Literature.
1987	*The Child in Time* awarded Whitbread Prize. Visited Soviet Union with delegation from END (European Nuclear Disarmament).
1988	*Soursweet*.
1989	Honorary D. Litt. from University of Sussex.
1990	*The Innocent*.
1992	*Black Dogs*.

Abbreviations and References

Page references to McEwan's works are to the Picador editions listed in the Select Bibliography.

AA   Christopher Ricks, 'Adolescence and After', *Listener* (12 April 1979), 526–7.

IG   *The Imitation Game: Three Plays for Television* (London: Pan Books/Picador, 1982).

MA   *A Move Abroad: Or Shall We Die? and The Ploughman's Lunch* (London: Pan Books/Picador, 1989).

NI   John Haffenden, *Novelists in Interview* (London: Methuen, 1985), 168–90.

PP   Rosa González Casademont, 'The Pleasure of Prose Writing vs Pornographic Violence: An Interview with Ian McEwan', *The European English Messenger*, vol. 1, no. 3 (Autumn 1992), 40–5.

PT   Christopher Ricks, 'Playing with Terror', *London Review of Books*, vol. 4, no. 1 (21 January – 3 February 1982), 13–14.

1

Introduction: The Art of Unease

Since the publication of his first book in 1975 Ian McEwan has sustained a reputation as one of the most exciting and controversial writers of his generation. The scandalous tales gathered in *First Love, Last Rites* won him instant critical acclaim and the Somerset Maugham Award for their precocious craft and originality. The appearance in 1978 of his compelling first novel, *The Cement Garden*, together with a second collection of remarkable stories, *In Between the Sheets*, confirmed the arrival of a singular, formidable new voice in modern British fiction.

Nor did McEwan take long to demonstrate the diversity of his talents. He achieved notoriety in 1979 when the BBC decided to suspend production of his play *Solid Geometry* on the grounds of its supposed obscenity. But with the success of his powerful script for *The Imitation Game* the following year he secured recognition as a television dramatist of manifest distinction. After completing his chilling second novel, *The Comfort of Strangers* (1981), which was shortlisted for the Booker Prize, McEwan struck out into new territory yet again, winning the Evening Standard Award for Best Screenplay for *The Ploughman's Lunch* (1983). As if this scathing portrayal of Thatcher's Britain were not sufficient proof of his versatility, the same year saw his libretto for Michael Berkeley's oratorio *Or Shall We Die?*, a passionate meditation on the threat of nuclear war, performed by the London Symphony Orchestra and Chorus.

Since then, apart from a brief collaborative excursion into children's fiction (*Rose Blanche*, 1985) and his admired screen adaptation of Timothy Mo's novel *Sour Sweet* (*Soursweet*, 1988), McEwan's main creative energies have been channelled into three

1

outstanding novels, which have both extended his range and deepened his vision: *The Child in Time* (1987), which was awarded the Whitbread Prize for Novel of the Year, *The Innocent* (1990), and *Black Dogs* (1992).

What is the nature of that vision, and how has it developed over the twenty-odd years in which McEwan has been writing? It is tempting to settle at once for the most obvious answer to that question, not least because it finds ample warrant in the evidence of the work itself. The received wisdom is that McEwan started out in the seventies as a writer obsessed with the perverse, the grotesque, the macabre. The secret of his appeal lay in his stylish morbidity, in the elegant detachment with which he chronicled acts of sexual abuse, sadistic torment and pure insanity. But towards the close of the decade his writing underwent a marked evolution as a result of his increasing involvement with feminism and the peace movement. His politically committed work for the cinema and television turned out to be a watershed in his career, from which his fiction emerged transformed. The claustrophobic menace of the stories and his first two novels gave way in the eighties to a more mature engagement with the wider world of history and society. The clammy feel of impending evil which fouled the atmosphere of his early fiction was dispelled by an emerging apprehension of the power of love and the possibility of redemption.

A familiar moral fable runs beneath this reading of McEwan's career. It casts the author as a kind of Prodigal Son, who gradually grows out of his nasty adolescent fantasies and into a responsible adult novelist. The story it tells looks suspiciously contrived and reassuring, but it is difficult to deny its plausibility as one reflects on the distance McEwan has undoubtedly travelled between the appearance of *First Love, Last Rites* and the publication of *Black Dogs*. There is an obvious sense in which a huge gulf does divide the suffocating themes and gothic mood of his earliest narratives from the widening scope and appetite for hope displayed by his more recent fiction. In an interview in 1983 McEwan himself identified *The Imitation Game* as the turning point, as a deliberate attempt to cast off his previous preoccupations:

> It was something I intended, because I had begun to feel rather trapped by the kind of things I had been writing. I had been labelled as the chronicler of comically exaggerated psychopathic states of mind

or of adolescent anxiety, snot and pimples. My relationship with Penny Allen, who is now my wife, was a rich source of ideas and I had wanted to give them shape. In writing *The Imitation Game* I stepped out into the world – consciously to find out about a certain time in the past and to recreate it – and at that point I felt I had made a very distinct change. (*NI* 173)

The importance of recognizing the scale of that change is underscored by the countless reviews of McEwan's recent novels which have ignored it, preferring to filter everything he writes through the demonic image he acquired from his first books. The headline over the review of *The Innocent* in the *Sunday Times* (6 May 1990) reads 'Sex, Death and Hidden Perversions'. McEwan is understandably vexed by the difficulty of shaking off this lurid caricature, because 'Once this set of expectations is set up round my work, people read it in this way. And even when, as in *The Child in Time*, there isn't this element, then *all* people write about is the absence of it. So, yes, I have a problem with my reputation and I give readings to try to oppose it, because I think that my work is not a monochrome of violence and horror' (*PP* 41).

But the myth of his devotion to depravity is not the only stereotype he has to contend with. Among those who registered the fact that his work had begun to part company with the deranged, and was climbing from the cellar into the sunlight, there were plenty eager to strap it into another straitjacket:

after writing *The Imitation Game* – having escaped the label of being the chronicler of adolescence – I was then suddenly the male feminist, which really made me shrink . . . I didn't want to be used as a spokesman for women's affairs. I didn't want to be a man appropriating women's voices. (*NI* 176)

Yet in some quarters this is exactly how he has continued to be seen. In *A Vain Conceit: British Fiction in the 1980s* (London, 1989) D. J. Taylor entitles his appraisal of McEwan 'Standing Up for the Sisters', tagging him 'the first male English writer to hook himself onto the feminist lobby' (p. 57). And in his polemical broadside *Venus Envy: On the Womb and the Bomb* (London, 1990) Adam Mars-Jones mocks McEwan as the bad boy who turned himself into the good father, into 'one of the few successful literary examples of the New Man' (p. 32), by hijacking the postures of the women's movement.

A failure to distinguish between early and later McEwan plays straight into the hands of those keen to label him solely as the sick delinquent confrère of Genet, Burroughs, and Céline or solely as the mature male feminist anxious to address the nation on matters of vital public importance. On the other hand, exaggerating the difference between the man who dreamed up *In Between the Sheets* and the man who penned *The Ploughman's Lunch* introduces other kinds of distortion. It either boils his career down to a gratifying tale of political enlightenment or it opens him to the charge of sacrificing art to moralism, of swapping the risks of the imagination for the safety of progressive pieties. That charge is one to which McEwan is rightly sensitive:

> I am aware of the danger that in trying to write more politically, in the broadest sense – trying to go out more into the world, because it is a world that distresses me and makes me anxious – I could take up moral positions that might preempt or exclude that rather mysterious and unreflective element that is so important in fiction. (*NI* 173)

And again:

> It's a minefield, politics and the novel. If you set about writing fiction with a clear intention of persuading people of a certain point of view, you cramp your field, you deny yourself the possibility of opening up an investigation or free inquiry . . . (*PP* 44)

Throughout his career McEwan has seen his writing as an act not of illustration but of exploration, as a way of questioning and even confounding the understanding from which he and his readers begin.

The focus of McEwan's work did shift dramatically after *The Imitation Game*. But the temptation to reduce his development to an exemplary tale of moral maturation or artistic depletion needs to be resisted. Such simplified accounts of his trajectory obscure the continuities and contradictions of his work. They screen off the intriguing ways in which the obsessions of the earlier fiction return to haunt the later writing, whose constructive engagement with history, society, and patriarchy is far from immune to the discourse of nightmare and despair. But they are equally blind to the moral and political implications of McEwan's early studies in deviance and transgression, which bristle with unsettling insights into problems of gender, power, and pleasure. What makes McEwan such an exciting writer to read is his appetite for the unpredictable and his readiness to cut the ground from under himself. A tale ostensibly remarkable only for its wilful obscenity and eccentric violence will unzip to disclose a sardonic critique of masculinity; while a screenplay or novel intent on edification will be sabotaged by its own confession of steep doubts and intractable anxieties. What binds all McEwan's books together is their power to unseat our moral certainties and sap our confidence in snap judgements. His writings are adventures in the art of unease, the art of playing havoc with the preconceived.

2

Growing Pains
First Love, Last Rites

Looking back on his short stories some years after he wrote them, McEwan once remarked: 'They were a kind of laboratory for me. They allowed me to try out different things, to discover myself as a writer' (*PP* 40). As the title of his first volume intimates, most of his earliest experiments involved a return to the bewildering experience of adolescence through which he had only just passed himself. In part it was simply a matter of tackling one of the few universal subjects of which he could claim painful first-hand knowledge. But adolescence also offered a unique standpoint from which to explore that elusive border country where guileless infancy and adult knowledge merge:

> adolescents are an extraordinary, special case of people; they're close to childhood, and yet they are constantly baffled and irritated by the initiations into what's on the other side – the shadow line, as it were. They are perfect outsiders, in a sense, and fiction – especially short stories, and especially first-person narratives – can thrive on a point of view which is somehow dislocated, removed. (*AA* 526)

The dislocated gaze of the adolescent robs adult behaviour of its transparent familiarity, while forbidding any sentimental retreat into the idealization of infancy. Seeing the world through the eyes of figures who feel equally alienated from innocence and experience throws into relief assumptions that might otherwise remain invisible and unexamined.

In 'Homemade', the opening story of *First Love, Last Rites* (1975), a cynical, self-regarding narrator, whose voice McEwan lifted from the braggart yarns of Norman Mailer and Henry Miller, recalls the night his teenage self disposed at last of his virginity.

The queasy twist to the familiar tale is that our hero's victim is his ten-year-old sister, Connie, whom he dupes into 'one of the most desolate couplings known to copulating mankind' (p. 24). Betraying not a flicker of compunction, he stalks his unsuspecting quarry like a wolf tailing a stray lamb. He lures Connie into his nasty homemade trap by suggesting her favourite game of Mummies and Daddies, the staple home-making fantasy with which she has been programmed: 'I was plunged into the microcosm of the dreary, everyday, ponderous banalities, the horrifying, niggling details of the life of our parents and their friends, the life that Connie so dearly wanted to ape' (p. 20).

On the face of it an account of the incestuous violation of a small child has little to recommend it. But the merely salacious possibilities of the story are subverted by the wicked black humour with which it mocks masculine postures and travesties the domestic script most adults wind up acting out. The narrator defies us to wax moralistic about a deed whose sordid enormity is eclipsed by his shameless thrill of triumph: 'I felt proud, proud to be fucking, even if it were only Connie, my ten-year-old sister, even if it had been a crippled mountain-goat I would have been proud to be lying there in that manly position, proud in advance of being able to say "I have fucked", of belonging intimately and irrevocably to that superior half of humanity who had known coitus, and fertilized the world with it' (pp. 23–4).

The passing of childhood in 'Last Day of Summer', by contrast, is suffused with an eery sadness and overshadowed by the deaths with which the narrative concludes. The opening sentence immerses us at once in the mentality of the juvenile narrator: 'I am twelve and lying near-naked on my belly out on the back lawn in the sun when for the first time I hear her laugh' (p. 41). The sustained present tense simulates the artless idiom of the boy, creating a poignant tension between the limits of his language and the momentous events whose implications he intuitively apprehends. The retrospective narrator of 'Homemade' was only too keen to press upon us his mature interpretation of his rite of passage. 'Last Day of Summer' draws its power from leaving its narrative unplaced and replete with unforced significance.

The nameless narrators of both stories do share, however, an incapacity to be appalled. When the bright green rowing-boat of boyhood capsizes on the last day of summer, huge fleshy Jenny and little baby Alice tragically drown and disappear. The orphaned narrator has been orphaned yet again by the loss of the woman who has become a second mother. But his response to their deaths as he drifts homeward, 'hanging on to the green shell with nothing in my mind' (pp. 54–5), is a curious blank detachment which refuses to register grief or horror. Lurking beneath the surface of the story is a sinister matricidal fantasy, cleansed of the guilt which would cling to the wilful murder of an actual mother. The embodiment of maternity must be sacrificed so that the man may survive, isolated and anaesthetized, to enter the wintry world symbolized by school and the looming metropolis toward which the river sweeps his abandoned boat.

'Last Day of Summer' is a parable about the cruel cost of turning into a man. Becoming masculine means a murderous denial of the dependency and need for intimacy evoked by the mother and the female body. Learning to fear the feminine and deep-freeze the emotions is a condition of fashioning the kind of adult male identity most cultures promote. But the self forged by this act of repression is fragile, and constantly assailed by insurgent drives to restore the very state masculinity must repudiate. In 'Conversation with a Cupboard Man' we meet the first of McEwan's many studies in infantile regression, as our interlocutor recounts the events which warped him into a reclusive freak curled up in his womb-like wardrobe. It is the hidden emotional history of many men, grotesquely caricatured as the confession of a madman. Until he is seventeen his widowed mother forces her only child to remain a baby, making him sleep in a crib, tying a bib round his neck, leaving him helpless and retarded: 'I could hardly move without her, and she loved it, the bitch' (p. 76). But his mother's remarriage terminates his childhood overnight and tosses him out into the cold to fend for himself as a man. The upshot is a volatile mixture of loathing for his mother, from whose oppressive nurture he was so cruelly divorced, and a consuming hunger to return to that blissful state of coddled impotence recovered in the cupboard: 'I don't want to be free. That's why I envy these babies I see in the street being bundled and carried about by their mothers. I want to be one of them. Why can't it be me?' (p. 87).

The frailty of masculine identity is also the subject of the last story in the collection, 'Disguises'. Like 'Homemade', this story revolves round the sexual abuse of a child, but in this case the victim is a ten-year-old schoolboy called Henry and the predator is his flamboyant aunt Mina – a thespian paedophile with a taste for transvestism. After his mother's death, Mina becomes what she calls 'a Real Mother' (p. 100) to her orphaned nephew, who is at first enchanted by her eccentric theatricality and her fantastic dressing-up games. But their relationship takes a sickening turn when Mina forces him to dress as a sweet little girl in party frock and wig, while she molests him in the uniformed guise of a dashing, drunken officer. As Mina presses the boy's face 'against the faintly scented corrugated skin of her limp old dugs', which appear 'grey and blue the way he imagined a dead person's face' (p. 116), his mind glimpses in the repulsive flesh of his surrogate mother the corpse of the mother he has lost.

Through his love for his schoolfriend Linda, however, Henry learns to translate the oppression of his costume into a source of pleasure and a refuge from guilt. His masculine shell dissolves and he becomes 'invisible inside this girl' (p. 114), blissfully released from the burden of identity and hence from the blame that a fixed self incurs: 'all disguised and no one knows who you are, anyone can do what they want because it doesn't matter' (pp. 117–18). The horror of letting go is coupled with a dionysiac delight in the effacement of borders and the violation of deep-seated taboos. The confounding of sexual difference and the suspension of liability are as enticing as they are frightening, and McEwan taps straight into our aptness to be torn by both emotions.

The fearful yet envious fascination of the male for the female, and for the maternal female in particular, surfaces again in the title story of the volume. As the teenage narrator makes summer love with his girlfriend, Sissel, he is gripped by an ecstatic sense of subjection to the ancient urge that pulses in every species: 'It was eggs, sperms, chromosomes, feathers, gills, claws, inches from my cock's end the unstoppable chemistry of a creature growing out of a dark red slime, my fantasy was of being helpless before the age and strength of this process' (p. 90). Their reproductive act is creepily answered by a scratching of claws behind the wall, the real claws of a pregnant rat which their coupling seems to have summoned into being: 'I knew it was my own creature I heard scrabbling . . . it was a sound which grew out of our lovemaking' (p. 91). The rat is acknowledged as their 'familiar' (p. 96), the incarnation of the drive which levels the distinction between rodent and man. The longing to slide out of human identity and cultural definition, to merge with the purely creatural, is powerful, and for a time the couple succumb, wallowing in their own filth and listless abjection. But entropy becomes intolerable too, so the mother rat must be brutally killed off: the border between man and animal must be redrawn by an act of violence, by a formal expression of disgust. In the very moment of the rat's destruction, however, its consanguinity with its killers is revoltingly confirmed:

> It dropped to the ground, legs in the air, split from end to end like a ripe fruit . . . A faint smell crept across the room, musty and intimate, like the smell of Sissel's monthly blood. Then Adrian farted and giggled from his held-back fear, his human smell mingled with the wide-open rat smell. I stood over the rat and prodded it gently with the poker. It rolled on its side, and from the mighty gash which ran its belly's length there obtruded and slid partially free from the lower abdomen a translucent purple bag, and inside five pale crouching shapes, their knees drawn up around their chins. As the bag touched the floor I saw a movement, the leg of one unborn rat quivered as if in hope, but the mother was hopelessly dead and there was no more for it. (p. 98)

The scene also involves another displaced murder of the mother, here transformed into a version vile enough to license her extermination by the adolescent male.

There is nothing figurative to mask the dreadful murder of a little girl described in 'Butterflies'. McEwan slips inside the lonely mind of a child-molester and imagines him remembering how he drifted, almost by accident, into assaulting and drowning the nine-year-old daughter of a neighbour. The details of the incident are distasteful enough, but their impact is aggravated by the narrator's impassivity: 'My mind was clear, my body was relaxed and I was thinking of nothing . . . I lifted her up gently, as gently as I could so as not to wake her, and eased her quietly into the canal' (pp. 72–3). Confronted with his victim's corpse by the suspicious police, he remains guiltless and unperturbed, compelled only to resist an impulse to touch her damp, dead body on the stainless-steel table.

The story is so disturbing because it invites us to identify exclusively with the paedophile's point of view and embrace his indifference to judgement. What makes such narratives hard to swallow is not so much the author's soft spot for the gruesome as his seeming content to withhold moral appraisal, to let the monstrous smuggle itself out of his unconscious duty-free. The celebrated clinical precision of McEwan's style is crucial to this effect. The contained, impersonal prose, purged of emotive resonance, works hand in glove with the nerveless narrators it is so often conscripted to serve. Its detachment administers the anaesthetic which allows the most loathsome acts to be probed without pain, in a context uninfected by sentiment or moralism.

The reluctance of most narrators in this volume to be named is another vital device for preserving the illusion of steely masculinity and keeping culpability at bay. The narrator of 'Solid Geometry' exploits his anonymity to explain how he disposed of his insufferable wife, Maisie, thanks to a mind-bending mathematical secret discovered in his ancestor's journal. Poor muddled Maisie craves affection and sex from her husband, who greets her overtures with icy contempt. The more she pleads, the deeper he retreats into the fortress of abstraction he has built in his study: 'I felt no desire for Maisie or any other woman. All I wanted to do was turn the next page of my great-grandfather's diary' (p. 33). Along with the diary, his eccentric forebear has bequeathed him the mighty twelve-inch member of the nineteenth-century rogue Captain Nicholls, which floats proudly in its glass jar on the narrator's desk. It is Maisie's angry smashing of this precious icon of sexual difference and male supremacy that seals her doom: 'Amid the broken glass and the rising stench of formaldehyde lay Capt. Nicholls, slouched across the leather covers of a volume of the diary, grey, limp and menacing, transformed from a treasured curiosity into a horrible obscenity' (p. 33).

The image vividly encapsulates the sense of masculinity in crisis which pervades the volume. But the narrator's response to this female attack on the sovereignty of his sex is equally exemplary and instructive. The fantastic means of revenge is aptly supplied by the diary, the symbol of his patriarchal heritage. The narrator summons 'the highest, most terrifying form of knowledge, the mathematics of the Absolute' (p. 37), to make Maisie vanish from the face of the earth. Under the cruel pretence of making love to her at last, he enlists pure, disembodied rationality to annihilate the menstruating, baby-making body that repels him. It is a clean, bloodless murder without a corpse, an elegantly austere solution which affords all the satisfaction of slaying without the messy guilt: 'As I drew her arms and legs through, Maisie appeared to turn in on herself like a sock... Then she was gone ... and not gone. Her voice was quite tiny. "What's happening?" and all that remained was the echo of her question above the deep-blue sheets' (p. 40).

As the stories in *First Love, Last Rites* attest, growing into a man means suppressing everything habitually identified with the mother and the feminine, everything which threatens to expose the brittle artifice of male autonomy. This includes the animal functions and processes of the human body itself, the levelling evidence of our shared biological being, of the physiological affinities that traverse and mock the distinctions of gender we impose. But the will to remain hard, clean, and contained is repeatedly undermined by the yearning to relapse into that abject ecstasy in which manhood evaporates and the whole system of differences on which patriarchy depends collapses in scandalous confusion. Hence the notorious itch of McEwan's fiction to revel in the disgusting, to dwell on the secretions and excretions of the human organism – the mucus and saliva and menstrual flux – which return us to the visceral reality of the flesh. But since the survival of patriarchal culture depends on the disavowal of the feminized flesh, maleness must be forced into being over and over again through acts and attitudes fuelled by hatred and fear, through a pathological obsession with keeping vulnerability at bay and concealing the abandoned child within. Time after time, in fantasy if not in fact, the mother must be killed off, the child must be violated, and the tell-tale body must be hidden away, to shore up the ramparts of a masculinity doomed to live under permanent siege.

3

Sex, Violence and Complicity

In Between the Sheets

One of the strengths of McEwan's stories is their willingness to address the implications of their unsavoury obsessions. Far from disguising the tainted pleasure they take in their more lurid themes, his best tales confess the ambiguity of their attitude and oblige us to reflect on the mixed motives governing our own response as readers. Given its persistent fascination with incest, paedophilia, sadism, cross-dressing and many other kinds of deviance and perversion, McEwan's early fiction not surprisingly attracted the charge of mere voguish nastiness. Asked to answer that charge in an interview with Christopher Ricks in 1979, McEwan replied: 'what is going to compel me into writing fiction is not what is nice and easy and pleasant and somehow affirming, but somehow what is bad and difficult and unsettling. That's the kind of tension I need to start me writing' (*AA* 526). It is also the kind of tension that keeps us reading narratives designed to disconcert us by poisoning the source of our satisfaction.

The title of the first tale in McEwan's second collection, *In Between the Sheets* (1978), seems eager to fulfil explicitly the oblique promise made by the title of the book itself. But 'Pornography' turns out to be the teasingly ironic title of a story which delivers more than we bargained for and in so doing throws the motives of author and reader into question. The narrative relates the fate of a sleazy pornographer's apprentice called O'Byrne, a callous sexual leech who two-times a couple of nurses and compounds the felony by infecting them both with the clap. Although he prides himself on his prowess as a lady-killer, the odious O'Byrne, whose fingers habitually exude a 'faint purulent scent' (p. 13), has made an alarming discovery while in bed with plump, domineering Lucy: he loves being violently abused and humiliated, and revels in his 'guilty thrill of pleasure' (p. 20) when she straddles him during sex, grips his throat in her hand and berates him as a 'dirty little worm' (p. 21). O'Byrne's secret craving lays him wide open to the meet revenge the nurses have in store, but it also imparts duplicity to the tale's horrifying climax.

Strapped to Lucy's bed and primed to enjoy his usual bout of masochistic bliss, our hero suddenly grasps that his paramours are about to amputate the offending member: 'We'll leave you a pretty little stump to remember us by' (p. 26). But as the sterilizer hisses on the bedside table and Lucy prepares the hypodermic, O'Byrne realizes what his erect penis already knows, that his terror is entwined with his fierce desire for this brutal violation. He wants the rapture of this terminal emasculation as intensely as he dreads it. Thus the story billed as pornography unfolds into a moral fable in which the lecherous male is punished, but in a way which fulfils his deepest sexual longing and converts the tale, perhaps, into a pornographic fantasy after all. The narrative wilfully blurs the distinction between morality and obscenity, insinuating that our appetites for both may be tougher to disentangle than we imagine.

McEwan is playing games – sometimes sardonic, sometimes dangerous games – with his and our addiction to sensationalized sex and violence, with our craven demand to be excited by garish transgressions. Sex and violence: the ubiquitous tabloid twins have become fetishized objects of consumer desire, and too many of us have acquired a taste for the illicit fix they deliver, whatever we may publicly and piously avow to the contrary. The pornographic is no longer skulking elsewhere, but happily tapdancing inside our heads. It has long since turned whole populations into voyeurs of staged and screened atrocities, greedy parasites on others' furtive pleasures, fatally deluding themselves that they are not answerable for the images on which they feed. Many of McEwan's stories are out to expose this insidious scenario by rattling the chains of complicity which bind writer and reader. They meet our demand for something shocking and salacious, but in a fashion which invites us to acknowledge our affinity with their estranged narrators and unhinged protagonists.

That invitation is overtly extended by the confessional posture of the first-person narratives, which cast the reader as confidant, as the secret sharer of what is divulged. The author throws his voice into a self licensed to feel and think and do all the disgusting, unspeakable things that arouse the reader too. The pleasure afforded both writer and reader is not confined to ironic superiority to the benighted narrator; it includes the vicarious pleasure of possession by one's own shameful double. Such fiction flagrantly panders to people's worst instincts, but its alertness to depravity's seductive appeal challenges its readers to come clean about the scale of their own capitulation. For as long as we keep fencing off the perverted and barbaric, the murderous and revolting, as unfathomably alien to us, the secret grip of these proclivities on our hearts only tightens. To admit to the delight we take in degradation, to find our own buried fantasies mirrored in the outcast's eyes, is to begin slackening the noose of blind compulsion.

'Dead As They Come' takes the form of a murderer's confession, decked out with as much sex and violence as that title, with its strident double-entendre, might lead one to expect. But this is McEwan country and the murderer is a crazed millionaire, whose passion for a dress-shop dummy ends with his strangling the lifeless object of his ludicrous fixation. Having convinced himself that the mannequin, his 'perfect mate' (p. 68), is betraying him with his chauffeur, he succumbs to a fit of vengeful rage and determines 'to rape and destroy her' (p. 76):

> Before she had time to even draw breath I was on her, I was in her, rammed deep inside while my right hand closed about her tender white throat. With my left I smothered her face with the pillow.
> I came as she died. That much I can say with pride. I know her death was a moment of intense pleasure to her. I heard her shouts through the pillow. I will not bore you with rhapsodies on my own pleasure. It was a transfiguration. And now she lay dead in my arms. (pp. 76–7)

One need only imagine these words applied to a flesh-and-blood woman to transform the ridiculous into the horrible, and take the point of McEwan's substituting this fetishized replica of a female. For this strategy allows us to hear the protagonist's entire monologue as a compendium of male clichés, and to recognize in his stereotyped fantasy the internalized script which leads men to treat women as things they own and kill them for real.

The story sends up the jaded, fatuous rhetoric of pornography, whose assumptions covertly dictate the plot of more sexual encounters than most care to admit: 'Between her thighs I caressed with my tongue the fetid warmth of her virgin lust. I took her hand and set her pliant fingers about my throbbing manhood' (p. 67). But the fun afforded by such parodic mockery does not preclude implicating the act of representation in which the tale itself is engaged. The narrator is also a collector of priceless paintings, and in the mannequin he sees 'beauty in another being as no man had ever seen it . . . it was art, it was the total consummation of line and form that art alone can realise' (p. 69). So when he destroys the dummy he destroys his collection as well: 'I made straight for the Utrillo and tore it to shreds . . . I tore, trampled, mangled, kicked, spat and urinated on . . . my precious possessions' (p. 77). The reification of women by the male gaze and the petrifaction of life in even great art may not be unrelated, involving as they both do the aesthetic reduction of the vital to an inert commodity.

'Reflections of a Kept Ape', which began life as a pastiche of Kafka's 'Lecture to an Academy', also enlists absurdity to sharpen its critique of stale sexual idioms and attitudes. The narrative is the forlorn ape's account of the end of his affair with his mistress, the best-selling novelist Sally Klee: 'We were lovers once, living almost as man and wife, happier than most wives and men' (p. 27). For a time Sally delighted in his simian strangeness, in his 'funny little black leathery penis' and the tea-like taste of his saliva (p. 29). But her flirtation with bestiality has since paled and her adoring anthropoid is left to mope ignored around the house, pining for his cruel mistress. The ironic gags are never funnier than when the monkey quotes from Sally's romantic novel the alleged profundities which betray its banality. But a less palatable humour leaks from the vivid physical details of sexual congress, which lend the fusion of human and animal a sensuous realism surpassing the requirements of mere travesty. Such touches collapse the distance on which the preservation of comic detachment depends, and the humour of incongruity gives way to an embarrassed glimpse of repressed kinship.

The poignant closing image compounds the discomfort by spinning the camera round to capture our own voyeuristic absorption in this erasure of disparity: 'Standing here behind Sally Klee I am struck by a vivid memory from my earliest infancy. I am staring at my mother who squats with her back to me and then, for the first time in my life, I see past her shoulder as through a mist pale, spectral figures beyond the plate glass, pointing and mouthing silently' (p. 41). What we are pointing and mouthing at is a bizarre cartoon of a stock romantic predicament, which turns the ghostly spectator into the creature in the cage. The tale drives home the chastening realization that strikes the boy in 'Last Day of Summer' as he watches a young mother squeeze the milk from her breast into a bottle: 'It made me think how we're just animals with clothes on doing very peculiar things, like monkeys at a tea party' (*First Love, Last Rites*, 49).

In *Between the Sheets* repeatedly stages scenes designed to dramatize uncomfortable questions of complicity. In 'Psychopolis', McEwan's much-admired tale of terminal alienation in LA, 'a city that existed only in the mind' (p. 126), the narrator's lover persuades him to chain her to his bed for a whole weekend and not release her under any circumstances. Although her bondage is voluntary and he is merely complying with her desire to toy with captivity, the narrator himself is hog-tied by his role in his girlfriend's mind-game. Her inevitable pleas for release, of whose seriousness he remains unsure, trap him in a dilemma which makes the experiment as much of a trial for him as it is for her:

> I was not at all excited. I thought to myself, If I unlock the chain she will despise me for being so weak. If I keep her there she might hate me, but at least I will have kept my promise. The pale orange sun dipped into the haze, and I heard her shout to me through the closed bedroom door. I closed my eyes and concentrated on being blameless. (p. 103)

But staying blameless is a tall order, requiring all one's powers of disavowal when responsibility is plain and absolution impossible. Later in the story the narrator is taken to a club where he watches an act intended to provoke a similar unease in the audience by confronting it with its capacity for denial and indifference. A bedraggled man who looks like a derelict, his jeans stained with real vomit, takes the mike and is greeted as a stand-up comic. But instead of gags he delivers a rambling, depressing monologue devoted to his own misery, which at first unsettles the audience and finally stops them listening altogether: ' "I've seen acts like that here," said Mary. "The idea, when it works, is to make your laughter stick in your throat. What was funny suddenly gets nasty" ' (p. 118).

It is the title story, however, which deals most directly with complicity as a condition of writing and a consequence of reading. In this tale of a father almost seduced by his own incestuous fantasies the reader is made to feel as incriminated as McEwan. The author is fingered as an accomplice by the fact that the protagonist, Stephen Cooke, is himself a writer. Nor does the narrator hesitate to draw parallels between Cooke's vampiristic qualities as a man and as an author. His sexual failure as a husband and his prowess as a writer are intimately allied. His ex-wife despises him for 'his passivity and for all the wasted hours between the sheets', for 'the experimentation in his writing, the lack of it in his life' (p. 88).

The story begins: 'That night Stephen Cooke had a wet dream, the first in many years' (p. 78). The dream discloses his subliminal lust for a prepubescent Italian girl who served him in a café, and it foreshadows feelings he is about to unearth for his own daughter, Miranda. Miranda herself appears to have a homoerotic relationship with her stunted schoolfriend, an eery 'doll-like figurine' (p. 85) who seems more like a knowing adult trapped in the body of a child. The narrative builds up an atmosphere suffused with the promise of forbidden satisfaction, exciting the reader's prurient empathy with this man whose libido remains locked in the nursery, safe from the grown-up demands of women.

The story flirts brazenly with pure pornography as it works up to a carnal encounter on the night Cooke's daughter and her friend come to stay. After seeing his daughter to bed, 'He sat down, horrified at his erection, elated' and 'waited for the chill of excitement to leave his belly' (p. 91). His feverish lust leads him to imagine orgasmic moans coming from the girls' room, and in a trance he steals naked to the bedroom door to listen. But what emerges from the room is simply his sleepless daughter in her nightdress, and the prowling paedophile vanishes back inside the tender father, who tucks his untainted child back into bed. The story brings him and us to the brink of a dreadful violation, only to swerve away at the last moment with a sobering realization of what had almost been destroyed, captured in a radiant image of innocence undefiled:

> But she was asleep and almost smiling, and in the pallor of her upturned throat he thought he saw from one bright morning in his childhood a field of dazzling white snow which he, a small boy of eight, had not dared scar with footprints. (p. 93)

18

4

Keeping Mum
The Cement Garden

McEwan's first novel returns us to the blighted Eden of adolescence explored in his earliest stories. *The Cement Garden* (1978) is the crucible in which the diverse obsessions of *First Love, Last Rites* are fused into a single hypnotic narrative. McEwan recalls clearly how the book began: 'It has a definite genesis in one paragraph of my notes, at the doodling stage, where I suddenly had a whole novel unfold about a family living "like burrowing animals . . . after mother dies the house seems to fall asleep"' (*NI* 170). The germinal idea is of a family of orphaned children reverting to a somnambulant state in which they dwell deep inside their home, marooned from reality, accountable to nobody, and released from the obligation to mature. 'I was trying to set up a situation where suddenly there were no social controls. Suddenly, children find themselves in the house – there are no teachers, no parents, no figures of authority, they have total freedom – and yet they are completely paralysed' (*AA* 526).

The claustrophobic old house itself is 'built to look a little like a castle, with thick walls, squat windows and crenellations above the front door' (p. 21). This desolate suburban fortress stands alone on an empty street, surrounded by a wasteland of rubble and burnt-out prefabs. Even before the parents expire the reclusive family boasts neither friends nor visitors; not even the milkman calls any more. Apart from the odd excursion into outlying streets, we stay sealed inside this secluded interior with this tight little knot of characters for the duration of the narrative. Once left to themselves, the children withdraw still further into physical and emotional recesses within their insulated domestic retreat. Their universe contracts into an increasingly confined space, which suffocates them but also secures them against the bleak, apocalyptic landscape beyond the walls.

The story revolves round the corpse of the mother, but it begins with the death of the father. The novel opens with a wry twinge of oedipal guilt: 'I did not kill my father, but I sometimes felt I had helped him on his way' (p. 9). Just as Jack, the fourteen-year-old narrator, ejaculates for the first time while masturbating indoors, his father obligingly drops dead outside, falling face-down in the wet cement with which he has begun to blanket the garden. But the implication that the son's accession to sexual potency has magically triggered the demise of his oppressive rival is left undeveloped. 'The little story of his death' (p. 9) is introduced as a preface to the real story that follows, and the first chapter of Jack's deadpan confession ends with the boy erasing the last physical trace of the man who sired him: 'I did not have a thought in my head as I picked up the plank and carefully smoothed away his impression in the soft, fresh concrete' (p. 18).

Wiping his mother from his thoughts proves a somewhat trickier task. When Mother finally dies in her bedroom after a painful, wasting illness, Jack persuades his siblings that the only way to prevent their being separated by the authorities is to conceal the fact of her death. They carry her body down to the cellar, place it in their father's huge tin trunk, and pour cement over it up to the brim. By this grotesque expedient they contrive to banish their dead mother from their minds and preserve her nevertheless as the invisible foundation of their lives. It has been remarked that Freud's vertical division of the human mind into superego, ego, and id bears an uncanny resemblance to the architectural structure of the late-nineteenth-century, middle-class home, which may have served as his subliminal model. Be that as it may, what the children enact in *The Cement Garden* gains immense allegorical resonance from McEwan's intuitive exploitation of this parallel. In bringing Mother's corpse down from the upstairs bedroom and burying it in the basement, the children physically enact the metaphorical interment of the lost mother in the unconscious.

Their action obeys a logic already rooted deep in Jack's mind. It is prefigured by two powerful images which surface before his mother's death. The first crops up in a bad dream Jack is woken out of when his mother enters his bedroom to warn him of the evils of self-abuse. In the dream someone is running after him to force him to look into a box: 'The lid was lifted half an inch or so, too dark to see inside . . . I knew there was a small creature inside, kept captive against its will and stinking horribly' (p. 26). The second occurs in the science-fiction novel Sue gives her brother for his fifteenth birthday. The story stars Commander Hunt, the intergalactic hero with whom Jack naturally identifies. The retrospective analogy between Hunt's mission and Jack's way of dealing with the remains of his mother is revealing:

> Minute life-bearing spores drifting in clouds across galaxies had been touched by special rays from a dying sun and had hatched into a colossal monster who fed off X-rays and who was now terrorizing regular space traffic between Earth and Mars. It was Commander Hunt's task not only to destroy this beast but to dispose of its gigantic corpse.
>
> 'To allow it to drift for ever through space,' explained one scientist to Hunt at one of their many briefings, 'would not only create a collision hazard, but who knows what other cosmic rays might do to its rotten bulk? Who knows what other monstrous mutation might emerge from this carcass?' (p. 34)

Jack's imagination has rehearsed the disposal of his mother's monstrous carcass; it is mesmerized by the prospect of putrescent flesh, and already torn between compassion and loathing for the creature that must be enclosed.

Despite Jack's parricidal act of erasure, the spirit of the father survives in the children's drive to entomb the maternal body within a pyramid of patriarchal roles and relationships. But there is also a violent aversion to entering the kingdom of the father and an irrepressible urge to linger in the empire of the mother, that balmy state in which the self still cleaves to the nurturing being from whose flesh it emerged. Indeed the burial of Mother in the basement trunk only enhances her power. Far from vanishing from her children's lives, she mutates like Commander Hunt's monster, becoming a gargantuan, enveloping presence. By secreting her body in the home, the children deny her death and protract her sway, deferring the demise of their own childhood. Their ghoulish act is a doomed attempt to make time stand still, to ward off the advent of growth and decay like Peter Pan. As Julie observes: 'I've lost all sense of time. It feels like it's always been like this . . . Everything seems still and fixed and makes me feel that I'm not frightened of anything' (p. 123). Yet the novel does not disguise the fact that this enchanted realm of arrested infancy is also a limbo of sluggish morbidity, which the children themselves feel drawn to destroy by restoring the structures of power and duty they have striven to subvert.

The gendered antagonisms at the heart of the novel are encapsulated in its oxymoronic title, with its apt evocation of a paved paradise, of organic vitality confronting lethal rigidity. But it is in the fate of the mother's body that these conflicts are most graphically inscribed. For her corpse is encased in the cement with which Jack's father had intended to smother their garden. The idea had been found strangely exciting by his son: 'Above all, mixing concrete and spreading it over a levelled garden was a fascinating violation' (p. 16). So when Jack later buries his mother beneath concrete in his father's old tin trunk, he is repeating the 'fascinating violation' devised by his father, using the tools and materials the latter has bequeathed him. But just as the father's attempt to petrify the garden is frustrated by his death, so the son's attempt to turn his Medusan gaze on his mother, to transform her into her own tombstone, is foiled by Mother's refusal to stay buried. The cement in the trunk expands and cracks, leaving the corpse visible and filling the house with the ominous stench that leads inexorably to discovery and to childhood's end: 'There was something sweet, and beyond that, or wrapped around it, another bigger, softer smell that was like a fat finger pushed into the back of my throat. It rolled up the concrete steps out of the darkness' (p. 108).

Before that moment of discovery, however, there is an unbridled interlude during which the law of the father struggles in vain against a reign of licence and confusion. When his mother dies, Jack realizes that 'beneath my strongest feelings was a sense of adventure and freedom which I hardly dared admit to myself' (p. 64). For a while he can wallow in the filth and apathy into which the household slides without the restraint of an adult figure of authority. He abandons hygiene and takes perverse delight in revolting his sisters with his greasy hair, filthy nails, yellowing teeth, and smelly feet. He drifts into a torpid daze of sleep, masturbation, and self-absorption. His incestuous lust for Julie, spawned in the furtive sex-games they played with Sue before their father died, thrives in this decadent climate and is eventually gratified. Jack's young brother Tom is likewise allowed to fulfil his fantasy by switching genders and reverting to babyhood. His sisters are only too pleased to abet his flight from masculinity and the march of time by dressing him as a little girl and treating him as a helpless toddler. Julie's metamorphosis into Tom's mother complicates matters still further by adding a seductive oedipal dimension to Jack's illicit desire for his sibling. For as long as the lawless interregnum lasts, conventional family roles are scrambled, sexual norms flouted and stable identities undone: 'Sometimes we were Mummy and Daddy and sometimes we were Julie and you and sometimes we were Julie and Derek' (p. 120). In this dissolute atmosphere of domestic entropy the children's grip on reality begins to go: 'every thought I had dissolved into nothing' (p. 81).

But even as Jack flounders spellbound in this quagmire of abjection, at once relishing and repelled by their debasement, he perceives that their unruly alliance has begun to duplicate familiar patterns of authority, to contract into a parody of the nuclear family they once were. Julie adopts the role of Mother to the rest, reducing Tom to his infant state in order to stress her power as head of the family. Jack at first plays the part of her sullen adolescent child, but towards the end acquires more respect and affection from her, as external threats to their fragile household bind them together like husband and wife. Julie does attempt to build a bridge into the outside world by introducing her adult boyfriend Derek into the family. But the intrusion of an outsider only underscores the impenetrable privacy of their universe, and Julie herself resists Derek's bid to take them under his wing: 'He wants to be one of the family, you know, big smart daddy. He's getting on my nerves ' (p. 122). By this point, though, there is no way back: the arrival of Derek heralds the destruction of their suburban bower of bliss.

The spell is broken when Julie and Jack make love in the complex scene which concludes their game of Mummies and Daddies. Yielding to the same regressive impulse as his brother, Jack climbs naked into the big cot beside Tom: 'The last time I had slept here everything had been watched over and arranged . . . lying in it now was familiar to me — its salty, clammy smell, the arrangement of the bars, an enveloping pleasure in being tenderly imprisoned' (p. 121). Julie is aroused by the sight of her brother in the posture of a baby, which casts her in turn as both mother and sister. Their intimate exchange sparks off an embrace which slides into coition, while baby Tom slumbers beside them. In quenching his lust for his sister, Jack consummates his desire for his mother, providing a suitably outrageous climax to the children's sustained assault on patriarchal law. But their initiation into adult sexuality as their virginity expires also marks an irrevocable break with the maternal universe in which they have been suspended. The baby in the crib beside them highlights the fact that they have begun playing Mummies and Daddies for real.

When Derek surprises them naked together on the bed, his horror and anger abruptly remind us how far the children have drifted from what custom defines as normality. After he storms out, they remain absorbed in each other's body and proceed to make love in a kind of trance, undaunted by his intrusion: 'Derek had been in the room such a short time that now it seemed as though we had imagined him' (p. 125). But Derek has gone down to the basement to smash the concrete tomb and expose the dead body of Mother. Jack and Julie make love to the rhythm of the sledgehammer as it shatters their cement garden:

> As I sucked and that same shudder ran through my sister's body, I heard and felt a deep regular pulse, a great, dull, slow thudding which seemed to rise through the house and shake it. I fell back and Julie crouched forwards. We moved slowly in time to the sound till it seemed to be moving us, pushing us along. (p. 126)

The sex act triggers the disclosure of the mother's death, which in turn cuts the umbilical cord at last, driving her offspring out into the grim adult universe. McEwan conveys the end of the idyll, as the forces of law irrupt into the children's closed world, with superb concision:

> It was the sound of two or three cars pulling up outside, the slam of doors and the hurried footsteps of several people coming up our front path that woke Tom. Through a chink in the curtain a revolving blue light made a spinning pattern on the wall. Tom sat up and stared at it, blinking. We crowded round the cot and Julie bent down and kissed him.
> 'There!' she said, 'wasn't that a lovely sleep.' (p. 127)

That image of bewildered infancy dazzled by the light of authority ensures that our relief at the children's release from enchantment is eclipsed by the sadness of their waking from the sleep of childhood, and by our knowledge that the real nightmare has barely begun.

5

Screen Tests
Jack Flea's Birthday Celebration,
Solid Geometry and
The Imitation Game

In his Introduction to *The Imitation Game: Three Plays for Television* (1981), McEwan explains that he started to write drama for TV in order to break out of the lonely business of writing fiction and try his hand at collaboration. But it was not only the prospect of company that attracted him. As a child of the television era he felt thoroughly at home with the naturalistic conventions of the medium, and confident enough to have a crack at taking them apart:

> Naturalism is the common language of television, not the language we speak, but one we are accustomed to. Simply by association it has become the language of the State, of an illusory consensus, and prone to all its contradictions. The centrality of television naturalism suggested, or so I thought, that formal experiment could therefore really matter, that by calling into question the rules of the common language the viewer could be disoriented and tempted to regard the world afresh. (*IG* 9–10)

By the time he came to write *The Imitation Game* (1980), McEwan had changed his mind about the limitations of naturalistic TV drama, realizing that what might prove a straitjacket in one context might provide bold opportunities in another for questioning the consensus. But his first two plays for television were conceived as 'attempts, however weak, to kick over the traces' (*IG* 10) by allowing the surreal to ride roughshod over the cosy laws of probability.

Jack Flea's Birthday Celebration (1976) was written in 1974, not long after McEwan completed the final story for *First Love, Last Rites*, and the play clearly belongs in subject and mood to that

25

volume. McEwan had a clear idea of what he was after: 'My intention was to take a television cliché – a kind of family reunion, a dinner party – and to transform it by degrees and by logical extension to a point where fantasy had become reality' (*IG* 11). The play's Pinteresque action is confined to the interior of the house in which David Lee, a boyish twenty-year-old, lives with a thirty-six-year-old schoolteacher called Ruth. David's parents have been invited to dinner to celebrate their son's birthday and to meet Ruth for the first time. As the evening wears on and the booze loosens tongues, the two women lock horns in a power-struggle over David, which David himself has stage-managed in order to wound and manipulate them:

MRS LEE. He might be living with you but he's still my son.
RUTH. No, no. He's my little boy now. I'm his Mummy now. (*IG* 40)

Ruth defiantly ties David's napkin round his neck like a bib and begins to spoonfeed him. The scene erupts into the bizarre spectacle of David playing the cartoon baby to the hilt – throwing food in his father's face, getting smacked and being soothed by Ruth as he starts to cry. But then Ruth and David collapse into laughter and the astonished Lees realize the whole thing has been a joke.

After they take their leave, though, one more twist is reserved for the viewer as the camera creeps into the bedroom for the closing scene. Ruth leans over David in close-up and kisses him passionately. But then:

We pull *away and see that* DAVID *is lying in a large cot.* RUTH *in a nightdress slides the side up, goes to the door, pauses there a moment to look at* DAVID, *smiles to herself, turns the light out and softly closes the door.*

A small night light burns. (*IG* 42)

The queasy blend of adult sexuality and infantile regression foreshadows the denouement of *The Cement Garden*. The play, like the novel, brings the subliminal to the surface by allowing its characters to act out a state of mind, to turn a figurative emotional plight into fact. McEwan dramatizes the fierce drive in women to reduce men to infants they can mother and control, but also the reciprocal eagerness of men to be unmanned and babied by the women in their lives. That the predicament is not merely David's eccentricity but a chronic disposition of the male gender is confirmed by the scene in which David's drunken father, left alone with his wife, kneels with his head in her lap to be comforted. Crippling patterns of behaviour are transmitted inexorably from one generation to the next, and internalized so completely that they become instinctive sources of gratification. If David is a victim, he is a victim who slyly connives at his own subjection and emasculation. This is intimated early on, in a scene before his parents arrive, when David is shown typing the title-page of the novel he has just completed, and we realize that the title is exactly the same as that of the play we are watching. The implication is that what transpires in the scenes that follow is scripted by David himself, conjured up by his own projections. This is borne out when David pretends to read the others a chapter from his novel called 'A Birthday Celebration', and prefaces his reading with a merciless sketch of the characters and situation before us. His psychological portrait of himself and Ruth, transparently disguised as Jack and Hermione, spares neither of them. The childless Hermione, he explains, 'decides to make Jack Flea her child, her fantasy child. It's a role that poor Jack Flea cannot resist. Hermione becomes his fantasy mother' (IG 33). The play builds its own pre-emptive interpretation into the script. It not only mocks the reductive reading it knowingly invites, but comes clean about its part in the conspiracy of repetition in which the characters are embroiled. This play knows that plays involve more than mirroring, that they are accountable for what they conjure into imaginative life, for the shapes they imprint on experience.

Solid Geometry (1979) is an adaptation of the short story discussed in chapter 2. In the interval between writing the tale in 1973 and reworking it for television five years later, McEwan's ideas about gender and power had become much more sharply defined, and that tightening of focus, that honing of intent, is immediately apparent in the revised TV version. McEwan went straight on from this script to research and write his overtly feminist play The Imitation Game. And when one reads the two plays in sequence their blatant incongruities of theme and style turn out to mask striking affinities. Solid Geometry emerges with hindsight as a kind of bridge between McEwan's first three books and the new territories mapped in The Imitation Game.

For one thing, the dramatization tilts the balance of sexual sympathy unambiguously towards the wife. As McEwan recalls, 'it was necessary to make Maisie as sympathetic as possible in her attempts to rescue the marriage; that way Albert's disposing of her would appear all the more callous' (*IG* 12). The script's instructions oblige the would-be mystic Maisie to be played as warm and loving, while Albert, the bloodless rationalist, must come across as 'self-absorbed' and 'eerily cold' (*IG* 49). The short story, by contrast, is told in the first person by the nameless husband, whose viewpoint and perception of Maisie the reader is tacitly invited to share. By depriving the narrator of his anonymity and naming him as Albert, the play objectifies him in our field of vision and exposes him to a judgement uncompromised by our complicity.

A further upshot of converting the tale into a teleplay is that the interrelation of past and present becomes more obvious and intriguing. The events recounted in Great-grandfather's diary, which the narrator of the story merely reports, must now be enacted in the play. McEwan's ingenious crosscutting of the nineteenth-century scenes and the modern episodes unearths parallels between the Albert/Maisie and Great-grandfather/Maxwell relationships which the narrative leaves buried. Both Albert and his ancestor, in their icy enslavement to abstraction, annihilate flesh-and-blood companions who insist, in Maxwell's words, that 'passion won't be reduced to numbers' (*IG* 57). The past locks the present into a cycle of replication so powerful as to collapse the gap of time dividing them.

The corridor that connects the generations in story and play is the diary. In the play its centrality is visually enhanced by dissolving from one time-frame to another through the glowing page of the book itself. As in *Jack Flea's Birthday Celebration*, McEwan is keen to stress the active role of the written word in creating and perpetuating coercive realities. In this case the textual transmission of secret power from one generation to the next secures male domination and the mentality prized by Albert and his precursor. Men's use of cryptic lore to shut women out and protect their sovereignty is a topic to which McEwan will return in *The Imitation Game*. Meanwhile, he has one last trick up his sleeve to embarrass the ideologically sound rationale of the script in the climactic scene. As Albert twists Maisie's limbs into an impossible configuration, McEwan's instruction reads: '*What takes place now between* ALBERT *and* MAISIE *must look as much as possible like a scene of lovemaking'*; and as Maisie is about to vanish, he notes: 'ALBERT *begins to turn* MAISIE *inside out. All the while he continues to kiss her.* MAISIE's *groans suggest the abandon of lovemaking, as well as fear and pain'* (*IG* 78). Maisie's agonizing extinction is also an orgasmic ecstasy, and the barbed suggestion is that more devious motives may be involved here than the play's neat polarities can cope with.

McEwan felt that *Solid Geometry* 'was, potentially at least, a far better play than a short story. It had a resonance and a life that had not been present previously' (*IG* 12). But a few days before it was due to be recorded the BBC halted production, citing the 'grotesque and bizarre sexual elements in the play' as the principal grounds for the ban. It now seems absurd that such reasons should have prevented a drama of such wit and invention making it to the small screen. After all, as Albert himself says to Maisie, 'it was only a prick in a pickle, wasn't it?' (*IG* 73). But perhaps the BBC intuitively perceived that more was at stake in the flaunted phallus than might meet the viewer's eye. When Maisie smashes the jar and exposes Albert's precious relic as a limp grey slug of putrid flesh, she unleashes the punitive wrath of a man who rightly feels that the root of his identity has been severed. In the guise of a surreal fable *Solid Geometry* blows the gaff on the frailty of male supremacy and shows the fate awaiting women who strike at the symbols of their own subjection.

Solid Geometry puts improbably what *The Imitation Game* unfolds all too plausibly through the tragedy of Cathy Raine. In this highly acclaimed play McEwan seats a woman at the centre of his work for the first time. His undisguised aim is to plug the movement for women's liberation into its past, to reinforce its historical authority by resurrecting the forgotten struggle of an earlier generation of women. McEwan had been deeply impressed by David Hare's trailblazing plays *Licking Hitler* (1978) and *Plenty* (1978), both of which concern the destructive consequences of a young woman's invasion of the world of men during the Second World War. Hare's inspiring example converged with McEwan's growing commitment to feminism to produce a play which shelved the obliquities of his previous work to grapple directly with 'the system whose laws, customs, religion and culture consistently sanction the economic ascendancy of one sex over another' (*IG* 14).

The Imitation Game is set in 1940, and tells the story of an ATS recruit who winds up at Bletchley Park, the home of the top-secret Ultra project designed to crack the German Enigma codes. While researching the play in the library of the Imperial War Museum, McEwan came across this exhortation from a wartime wireless broadcast and stitched it straight into the script as the epitome of the attitude Cathy crashes up against: 'Henceforward, as our colossal war machinery gets underway, no skilled person is to do what can be done by an unskilled person, and no man is to do what can be done by a woman' (*IG* 124). Cathy's refusal to submit to this routine denigration of her sex leads to increasingly serious clashes with authority – in her family, in the army, and in society at large – and eventually to her downfall at Bletchley. Because she knows herself capable of so much more than the menial chores to which she is relegated, she cannot resist pressing herself into situations where her will is bound to be frustrated and her safety imperilled. Eventually her ambition and curiosity take one risk too many. A romantic liaison with Turner, the brilliant young Cambridge don spearheading the Ultra operation, proves irresistible, because it offers a chance to steal into the centre of the labyrinth. Where she actually ends up is in jail, having discovered too much about Ultra to be left at liberty.

That, at least, is the official reason. In fact Cathy has discovered something far more sensitive and dangerous. When Turner's impotence transforms itself into vindictive rage against the witness of his weakness, she grasps the point of her sexual subordination and its relevance to the war. As she explains to the Colonel in her cell:

> If the girls fired the guns as well as the boys . . . if girls fired guns, and women generals planned the battles . . . then the men would feel there was no . . . morality to war, they would have no one to fight for, nowhere to leave their . . . consciences . . . war would appear to them as savage and as pointless as it really is. The men want the women to stay out of the fighting so they can give it meaning. As long as we're on the outside and give our support and don't kill, women make the war just possible . . . something the men can feel tough about. (*IG* 142)

Turner had flown into a fury because 'he couldn't bear to appear weak before me. He just couldn't stand it. Isn't that the same thing? I mean . . . as the war' (*IG* 143). The real top secret is the same one betrayed by *Solid Geometry*. Not only the war, but a whole social order and its system of values depend on enforcing sexual difference and the heterosexual hierarchy. Hence the importance of Turner's 'imitation game', which gives the play its title. The point of the game is to determine whether machines can think like human beings. What is telling is its adoption of the capacity to distinguish a man from a woman as its essential criterion of intelligence. As the game develops, however, it raises the troubling possibility that, since gender can be simulated, it is not an innate human property at all, and that nothing essential divides the sexes. The play itself is thus a form of the game, in as much as Cathy Raine blurs distinctions to the point where she rocks the foundations of the patriarchal edifice.

The Imitation Game undoubtedly stacks the deck in favour of the female victim of male cruelty. At the same time, there is a voyeuristic detachment about our point of view which suggests that another kind of story may lurk in the shadow cast by the play's feminist vision. When the play is watched with *Solid Geometry* in mind, it is disturbing to see how close it comes to implying the reverse of what is intended. The plot sets up a dissident woman to be isolated, helplessly snared in a web of male power, and finally entombed without appeal in prison. The empathetic portrayal of Cathy's heroic defiance harbours a darker fantasy in which the predatory eye of the camera stalks a lone female to her doom. This Jekyll-and-Hyde quality makes *The Imitation Game* more precarious and more truthful than a drama simply recycling the predictable feminist pieties. Not the least intriguing feature of McEwan's writing is that it knows it has a sinister side and is not prepared to disguise the fact, even if its progressive credentials end up muddied in the process.

The ambiguity of *The Imitation Game* emerges forcefully in the closing seconds of the play:

COLONEL. You're a very, very silly girl.
The cell door slams shut behind the COLONEL.
Cathy takes from the paper bag the score of K475.
She opens it and begins to read.
We read over her shoulder.
Fade in the piece itself, as played by Ivan Moravec.
We watch Cathy from a jailer's point of view – through the barred window of her cell. (IG 143)

31

Throughout the play Cathy's aspirations have found coded expression in her efforts to master Mozart's *Fantasia, K475*. So in this last scene we at once identify with her ('We read over her shoulder') as we hear the melody of her undaunted spirit still playing in her mind; yet we also watch her finally from the viewpoint of the jailer, gazing in rather than out through the bars. It is a disquieting moment, which puts our motives as viewers, as spectators of persecution, on the line. While our high-minded ideals are appeased by indignation at the injustice visited upon innocence, what atavistic appetites are being fed by this televised scapegoating of a deviant individual, which culminates in her graphic exclusion from the rest of us on this side of the screen?

With McEwan there is always something else brewing between the lines to complicate the immediate point of the story or play. It is this readiness to allow a work's unruly implications to invade and even usurp its ostensible intent that makes McEwan a writer who can be relied on to risk being honest, to deliver unpalatable truths instead of soothing delusions. And nowhere is his honesty more discomforting than in *The Comfort of Strangers*.

6

Coming Clean
The Comfort of Strangers

McEwan began *The Comfort of Strangers* (1981) about a year after finishing *The Imitation Game*. The novel took off from some notes he had made following a trip to Venice with Penny Allen in 1978. In the notes, he had already begun to describe 'two characters who were not quite like either myself or Penny', and to depict 'the city in terms of a state of mind, and vice versa' (*NI* 177). He set out, nevertheless, with no clear idea of where the book was heading and 'found it terribly difficult to write' (*NI* 178). One reason for the difficulty was intensely personal: 'I felt very strongly identified with Colin, as if I was writing my own death in some strange way. I felt terribly sickened by it' (*NI* 183). But another reason became more evident in retrospect. What he was uncovering as he wrote were needs and drives in men and women which made a mockery of the glib critiques of patriarchy still mouthed by countless right-minded individuals.

The Imitation Game had allowed itself a sideways glance at the crueller, ancient drama shadowing its every step; *The Comfort of Strangers* turns to look its demons in the face. No doubt the naturalistic form and idiom of the television play had imposed limits on what could be perceived and displayed. For in order to tackle the realities of sex and power, as McEwan had since come to realize,

> it wasn't enough to talk about men and women in social terms, I had to address myself to the nature of the unconscious, and how the unconscious is shaped. It wasn't enough to be rational, since there might be desires – masochism in women, sadism in men – which act out the oppression of women or patriarchal societies but which have actually become related to sources of pleasure. (*NI* 178)

However appalled the politically correct might be by the notion that sexuality is not at the beck and call of even the enlightened mind, but is swayed by murkier currents of need, McEwan's contention is that we cannot begin to think straight about power relations between the sexes until we own up to what actually excites and pleases us, until we stop talking as if reasoned argument alone were enough to transfigure the lineaments of desire.

The Comfort of Strangers traces the horrifying fate of a man and a woman who have screened off their true natures, and thus are left at the mercy of their own repressed appetites. Colin and Mary, a young English couple whose love has lost its edge and zest, are on holiday in Venice, cocooned in that languid atmosphere of numbed distraction McEwan has no equal in evoking. Late one night they meet the charismatic Robert, a pathologically virile native of the city. The latter exerts on them, in Christopher Ricks's apt phrase, 'the lethal hypnosis which the snake bends upon the rabbit' (*PT* 13). Robert's erotic obsession with the feminine Colin conspires with his guilty loathing of this affront to masculinity to seal Colin's fate. The strangely compliant Colin and Mary are lured into a trap in which Robert, with the connivance of his wife Caroline, fulfils his sadistic fantasies. He kisses Colin's blood-smeared lips, then calmly murders the object of his fixation as the drugged Mary watches in impotent terror. ' "See how easy it is," he said, perhaps to himself, as he drew the razor lightly, almost playfully, across Colin's wrist, opening wide the artery. His arm jerked forward, and the rope he cast, orange in this light, fell short of Mary's lap by several inches' (p. 121).

What makes the story so unnerving is the couple's passive collusion in this atrocity. Timing and circumstances combine to dismantle their psychological defences and expose their vulnerable inner selves. The fact that they are abroad in an alien environment, isolated in their hotel room from the routines and fixtures of their life back home, accelerates their dislocation from their normal identities. It is as if they have fallen into a trance, a nightmarish reverie whose insidious logic they have no choice but to pursue to its conclusion. Their mental and emotional derangement is compounded by their physical disorientation in Venice: their maps prove useless and they wander aimlessly around the city, constantly losing themselves in its maze of narrow, gloomy streets.

Our impression of their being adrift in the blurred ambience of a dream is heightened by McEwan's never stating explicitly that they are in Venice and never naming the celebrated locations through which the characters pass. We readily infer where we are, but the withholding of authorial confirmation leaves everything subtly uncertain.

No less disquieting is the suppression of the protagonists' surnames, which inflicts on the reader (to quote Ricks again) 'the discomfort of being lured into an unknowing intimacy with strangers, into a meeting-place which is fiercely lit and surrounded by shadows' (*PT* 13). Of Colin and Mary we learn enough to recognize in them a familiar kind of modern, metropolitan couple. She is divorced with two children and, although they are an established couple, they prefer to remain unmarried and choose not to live together. There is a fashionably epicene quality about them both, a degree of semblance sufficient to suggest the effacement of difference: 'When they looked at each other they looked into a misted mirror' (p. 18). Mary was for a time involved in a radical-feminist theatre company; Colin was once an actor and has qualified sympathy with Mary's feminist convictions, about which they often argue. Both obviously regard themselves as principled individuals who hold progressive views on questions of sexual politics.

In chapter 2 Mary stops at the window of a department store to examine with distaste a bedtime tableau illustrating the tenacity of patriarchal roles and assumptions. The postures of the male and female dummies and the gendered distribution of household props typify everything from which Mary and Colin recoil. Turning in anger from this shrine of sexual clichés and the rigid effigies at its centre, 'their arms and legs raised uselessly, like insects surprised by poison' (p. 23), Mary is delighted to come across the fly-posted manifestos of a militant feminist group. She pauses to read them, noting with approval that these Italian women are more radical than their English counterparts, and applauding their demand that convicted rapists be castrated.

Within moments they encounter the man who will put the credibility of such sentiments to the test. Robert may be the incarnation of all that Mary and Colin repudiate, but when he materializes from the shadows to appropriate them, we are left in no doubt that there is nothing accidental about their meeting. It later transpires that Robert had targeted Colin and stalked the couple from the start. But somehow, at a depth of awareness they prefer not to plumb, Colin and Mary have been expecting him too. In chapter 1 we are told: 'They used expensive, duty-free colognes and powders on their bodies, they chose their clothes meticulously and without consulting the other, as though somewhere among the thousands they were soon to join, there waited someone who cared deeply how they appeared' (p. 13). And when Robert does finally crystallize before the couple, they seem to have conjured him up like some malign genie:

> She pointed at a doorway several yards ahead and, as if summoned, a squat figure stepped out of the dark into a pool of streetlight and stood blocking their path.
> 'Now look what you've done,' Colin joked, and Mary laughed. (p. 26)

Robert and Caroline are not so much a threat from without as the enemy within; they are less the monstrous antithesis of our hero and heroine than their secret sharers, their untethered alter egos.

At first glance, however, the contrast seems total. When Mary lingers over another feminist proclamation on their way to his bar, Robert explains apologetically:

> 'These are women who cannot find a man. They want to destroy everything that is good between men and women.' He added matter-of-factly, 'They are too ugly.' Mary watched him as she might a face on television.
> 'There,' Colin said, 'meet the opposition.' (pp. 27–8)

They could hardly have been waylaid by a grosser caricature of macho posturing than this hirsute medallion man with his transparent black shirt split to the waist. But Robert's chauvinism is the legacy of a far from uncouth upbringing. He is the scion of a cultured diplomat, an authoritarian patriarch who instilled in his son through fear and punishment the same fanatical devotion to a strict ideal of masculinity that his own father had driven into him. Robert's early biography is an object lesson in how to mangle a gentle child who adores his mother into a sadistic misogynist and closet homosexual who cripples his wife for life.

Robert, of course, views his rearing as the cultivation of a real man like his father and grandfather: ' "They were men, and they were proud of their sex. Women understood them too." Robert emptied his glass and added, "There was no confusion" ' (p. 72).

Whereas nowadays, he maintains, men hate themselves and women do not respect them, because

> 'Whatever they might say they believe, women love aggression and strength and power in men . . . And even though they hate themselves for it, women long to be ruled by men. It's deep in their minds. They lie to themselves. They talk of freedom, and dream of captivity.' (p. 72)

His own wife is a limping testimony to the truth of his contention. She can imagine nothing more exalted than suffering utter agony and even death at the hands of the man she loves. As Caroline expounds to an incredulous Mary her creed of blissful subjection, an ocean of altered attitudes and ideals seems to divide the couples. Both women and both men appear to belong not simply to different generations and cultures, but to different galaxies.

Which is why Colin and Mary are so startled to discover, on their return from visiting Robert and Caroline, that their desire for each other has been rejuvenated and infused with a new kind of excitement. They begin to fantasize aloud about bondage and brutality, and find themselves unexpectedly enthralled by their latent dreams of domination:

> They took to muttering in each other's ear as they made love, stories that came from nowhere, out of the dark, stories that produced moans and giggles of helpless abandon, that won from the spellbound listener consent to a lifetime of subjection and humiliation. (p. 81)

Ominously, however, 'They did not discuss their stay with Robert and Caroline' (p. 79). Although their sexual renaissance inspires them to converse afresh about everything else, 'they could not talk about the cause of their renewal' (p. 81). It is a telling echo of the evasion noted at the beginning of the novel, long before they have run into Robert and Caroline: 'When they talked of the politics of sex, which they did sometimes, they did not talk of themselves' (p. 18). This is the crux of the matter, this 'unacknowledged conspiracy of silence' (p. 91), which sucks them towards the hideous denouement they covertly seek. As Mary admits to Caroline on their last fatal visit: 'We didn't exactly plan to come, but it wasn't completely accidental either' (p. 106). And just before Colin is murdered, Caroline tells the petrified victim: 'Mary understands. I've explained everything to her. Secretly, I think you understand too' (p. 119).

Colin and Mary become mesmerized by Robert and Caroline

for reasons they dare not admit to themselves or each other. Their own buried cravings induce them to acquiesce in their hosts' terrifying fantasy. As McEwan has commented:

> What is interesting is the extent to which people will collude in their own subjection, which is true not only of Caroline in relation to Robert but also of Colin. There is something about Colin's behaviour which suggests from the beginning that he is a victim; he goes along with Robert and is easily manipulated, which suggests an unconscious contractual agreement. I think such an agreement can exist between oppressor and victim . . . I did think there was a sense in which Colin and Mary had agreed about what was going to happen to them. (*NI* 181)

The unflinching honesty of *The Comfort of Strangers*, its refusal to offload the usual cant and sustain the conspiracy of silence, makes it a bleak but bracing book to read. It provokes us to wrestle afresh with the fear that 'the sexual imagination, men's ancient dreams of hurting, and women's of being hurt' (p. 125) may not be so amenable to transformation as we might wish. The age-old conundrum will not go away: how much of what we desire is the product of arbitrary cultural impositions, the transient concoction of historical circumstance, and how much belongs to a timeless realm of instinctual necessity which laughs at our attempts to escape its clutch or deny its endurance?

McEwan is far from relinquishing the belief that much of what poisons human relations can be laid at the door of that specific cultural formation known as patriarchy. The possibility that sexual violence and injustice might eventually be eroded along with the structures and ideas that fostered them is by no means ruled out. On the contrary, the detailed history we are given of Robert's formative years supports the inference that men like him are made rather than born that way, and a seed of hope blossoms in that conclusion. At the same time, the roots of Colin's and Mary's thirst for victimization are left quite unexamined; no case history is entered to account for what dwells uninvited within them. By the time Colin is bleeding to death on Robert's floor, appeals to the malign sway of patriarchy fall some way short of explaining what possesses these people, and the psychobiography of Robert looks altogether too neat and intelligible.

In the end *The Comfort of Strangers* capitulates to neither view of the matter, staging instead an unfinished dialogue between them. The conflict at the heart of the novel is inscribed from the start in the tension between the epigraphs that preface the narrative. The first is taken from a poem by Adrienne Rich, and it signals the novel's engagement with a feminist understanding of what ensues: 'how we dwelt in two worlds/ the daughters and the mothers/ in the kingdom of the sons'. But the second, from Cesare Pavese, which plainly suggested the title of the novel, incites us to wonder whether this book is about to broach matters that lie beyond the reach of historical understanding and social critique:

> Travelling is a brutality. It forces you to trust strangers and to lose sight of all that familiar comfort of home and friends. You are constantly off balance. Nothing is yours except the essential things – air, sleep, dreams, the sea, the sky – all things tending towards the eternal or what we imagine of it.

The novel which follows leaves us poised between the implications of both epigraphs. It knows that the argument between the outlooks they suppose is far from over yet, and is not afraid to intimate that it may well never be.

7

In Time of Fear
Or Shall We Die? and *The Ploughman's Lunch*

The Comfort of Strangers inevitably raises awkward questions about the nature of the novelist's art and its relation to his politics. McEwan's most sustained reflections on these matters occur in his Preface to *A Move Abroad* (1989), the volume which yokes together *Or Shall We Die?* (1983) and *The Ploughman's Lunch* (1983) as consciously committed endeavours. There he insists on the need for a novel to be an unpredictable act of exploration, which puts its author's and readers' preconceptions to the test of the narrative imagination: 'even with the most rigorous of schemes at your elbow, the best writing, the real discoveries and almost certainly the greatest pleasures will come from precisely what is unplanned' (*MA* ix). Nothing could be more inimical to the inquiring spirit of the true novelist than the grinding of some ideological axe or the thumping of theoretical tubs: 'The difficulty and conflict arise when the novelist has designs on his readers' opinions before anything is revealed. The novel then risks becoming not an exploration or investigation, but an illustration of conclusions already reached, the fleshing out of abstractions' (*MA* x). So, as the creative act of narration begins, those conclusions and abstractions, however noble and incontestable they may seem, have to be held in abeyance: 'You enter a state of controlled passivity, you relax your grip and accept that even if your declared intention is to justify the ways of God to man, you might end up interesting your readers rather more in Satan' (*MA* xi).

This is not to say that effective fiction has nothing to do with politics. It is rather that it refuses to take established positions and programmes at their own estimate, however attractive and convincing they appear. For that very reason a good novel may be of immense political value in a less obvious sense, in so far as its scepticism resists the sway of ossified opinion, forcing readers to reappraise what has congealed into doctrine. It is by eschewing political engagement in the obtrusive, narrow sense that the novel may succeed in redefining what counts as political, may clear a space in which a genuinely transformative politics, purged of self-deception, may take shape.

Nevertheless, there are times and places for writing which does serve more urgent and specific ends, which frankly sets out to exhort and enlist. In such works the author's eloquence and invention are placed at the service of controversy rather than dispatched on a voyage of discovery in which proclaimed allegiances are suspended. There is no reason, however, why the discourse of commitment should not flow into the novel and suffer there a sea-change into something richer and stranger. This is what happens with *The Ploughman's Lunch* and *Or Shall We Die?* Both works were protesting responses to particular situations in the early 1980s, and they both meant 'a move abroad' for their author in as much as they were 'flights from, or tactical evasions of, novel writing'; yet at the same time, as McEwan notes, 'these two pieces were the groundwork for the novel I began in 1983, *The Child in Time*' (*MA* vii).

McEwan wrote the libretto for Michael Berkeley's oratorio in 1982 in a climate of mounting international tension and intensifying private fear, as the superpowers stepped up the arms race and the world held its breath. The apocalypse which once seemed a remote contingency had become an all too plausible scenario, provoking mass popular demonstrations in both Europe, the likely theatre of nuclear war, and the United States itself. It was the impact of the pervasive mood of suppressed panic on ordinary individuals, and especially on parents terrified for their children, that moved McEwan to express directly what was at stake at this moment in world history. What attracted him to the form of the oratorio was the chance it offered to dramatize the plight of the species and plead for its salvation with a pure emotional force he could not otherwise command: 'No characters, no psychology, no actors pretending to be other people, simply voices articulating profoundest fears and some hope' (*MA* 6).

At the core of the libretto is a vision of humanity imperilled by the latest phase of the eternal war between the male and female principles, a war waged as much within individuals as in society at large. Science and the state, the makers of bombs and the makers of laws – all 'Diligent, logical, disciplined men' who claim to defend 'order, freedom, property, sovereignty, the aspirations of the people' (MA 20) – have conspired to bring their own kind and the planet itself to the brink of extermination. 'Our virile times' can take all the credit for

> the conquest of nature, the slaughter of species,
> the burning of forests, the poisoning of ocean and air,
> the tyranny of scale, the weapons, the weapons.
>
> (MA 23)

Everything that resists the forces of oblivion is fused into the image of a mother and her child, the epitome of what civilization seeks to protect and the symbol of qualities without which our doom is sealed. In the opening song of WOMAN, the nurturing maternal impulse and feminine compassion are indivisible from a simple delight in nature's elemental beauty:

> A nightjar sang. In the house below
> my daughter slept. By her window was a tree.
> A fresh wind stirred its leaves. My joy
> engulfed the house, the land on which it lay,
> the dome of infinite stars.
>
> (MA 17)

'It is as if nuclear energy is a kind of evolutionary filter', writes McEwan in his Introduction to the libretto. 'Of those civilisations who make the discovery, only those who do not build the weapons or, less likely, build them and do not use them, survive to evolve further' (MA 8). Mankind is submitting to the supreme test of its biological viability, and whether we pass the test depends on whether masculine or feminine values ultimately prevail. The choice is as stark as that: 'Shall there be womanly times, or shall we die?' (MA 23).

The oratorio leaves us impaled on the anxiety of that question, acutely aware that things are so grim that it might well be too late, but roused for just that reason into opposition. After all, as the

Preface reminds us, 'Pessimism is just one of morality's techniques' (*MA* xvi); or in the words of the libretto: 'Only shadows point the way' (*MA* 24). We can perhaps take heart too from the fact that the same scientific revolution that produced the bomb also ushered in a fresh way of thinking about the universe and our place in it that may ultimately prove our deliverance. Just as the Newtonian world-view gave way to the new physics, so the positivistic, masculine mentality it bred may be poised to surrender to a more feminine acceptance of subjectivity and uncertainty. If this is so, the human race stands at the threshold of an epoch in which the destructive antagonisms between the isolated self and the community, the subject and the external world, intellect and feeling, science and morality, could at last be overcome. At present 'Our science mocks magic and the human heart,/ our knowledge is the brutal mastery of the unknown' (*MA* 23). But a world which had undergone the 'evolutionary transformation of consciousness' (*MA* 15–16) envisaged by McEwan would be one content to declare: 'The planet does not turn for us alone./ Science is a form of wonder, knowledge a form of love' (*MA* 24). The prospect is, of course, wildly utopian: 'To desire a given outcome is not sufficient reason for believing it will transpire. If we are free to change, then we are also free to fail' (*MA* 16). But the libretto's dream of what we could become is as vital to our drive for survival as its glimpse of how close we are to the edge of the cliff.

By contrast, the depiction of Britain in *The Ploughman's Lunch* leaves little that is positive to latch on to. When the radical right-wing populism preached by the Thatcher administration took hold of Britain in the early eighties, the moral climate of the country underwent a violent transformation. Within a couple of years all the old decencies appeared to have died off, leaving people to fend for themselves in a vicious Darwinian culture:

> Money-obsessed, aggressively competitive and individualistic, contemptuous of the weak, vindictive towards the poor, favouring the old American opposition of private affluence and public squalor, and individual gain against communal solutions, indifferent to the environment, deeply philistine, enamoured of policemen, soldiers and weapons – virile times indeed. (*MA* xxiv)

In the film the few characters who swim against the tide of selfishness and cynicism are rapidly exposed as self-deluded or so impotent and marginal as to seem merely eccentric. But grafting gratuitous optimism onto his narratives has never held much appeal for McEwan. *The Ploughman's Lunch* delivers a comfortless vision of national and personal corruption feeding off each other in a lethal symbiosis, while history and memory are sacrificed to lies and myths, to convenient fabrications of the public and private past.

The film unpacks an episode in the life of James Penfield, a BBC news editor who sets out to write a book revising the standard view of the Suez crisis of 1956. His aim is to reinterpret Britain's treachery and humiliation as a justified, even honourable attempt to defend the remains and ideals of Empire, and the conduct of Eden's government as something to look back on with pride rather than mortification. At the same time James is in vain pursuit of the glamorous but shallow TV researcher Susan Barrington, who embodies the elite lifestyle to which he aspires. To win her he is prepared to deny his past, disown his family, and shamelessly exploit whoever comes to hand. The symmetry of the two enterprises is unmissable. As James doctors Britain's past to suit the spirit of the eighties, he unwittingly enacts in his personal life a series of betrayals and deceptions which mirror the public events he is distorting in his history.

Ironic parallels likewise abound between the Suez débâcle and the Falklands crisis, which broke while McEwan was working on the script. The film keeps us posted throughout on the progress of the war, deftly splicing updated allusions into the personal history of the protagonist, for whom the conflict means nothing but confirmation that he is riding the right bandwagon. In the climactic scene of the film, for which the crew and cast cheekily smuggled themselves into the 1982 Conservative Party Conference at Brighton, James realizes that he has been gulled by Susan and his best friend precisely as Mrs Thatcher makes her celebrated triumphal speech to Conference:

> The spirit of the South Atlantic was the spirit of Britain at her best. It has been said that we surprised the world, that British patriotism was rediscovered in those spring days. Mr President, it was never really lost! (*MA* 115)

It is a beautifully timed and crafted moment. The Prime Minister's speech exploits the same obsolete rhetoric and spurious sentiments that fuelled the Suez affair, the fiasco which signalled the end of Britain's imperial reign and exposed its grandiose self-image as a tattered illusion. And as the half-baked Churchillian sound-bites ring round the hall, the man who is breathing the spirit of the South Atlantic back into the Suez story winds up as duped and degraded as the nation was in 1956, when it was fed the same pernicious twaddle as it is being asked to swallow again in 1982.

All the main characters are involved in one way or another in representing the nation, in moulding our perception of its identity. James works at the hub of the national news service and is writing a history textbook; his louche friend, Jeremy, is a political journalist; Susan is researching a documentary series on modern world history; Susan's mother, Ann, whom James callously uses and dumps, is a distinguished left-wing historian; and her philandering husband, Matthew, is a successful director of TV commercials. It is Matthew, appropriately, who explains the title of the film. As a preface to giving James permission to sleep with his wife, he illustrates Britain's supremacy in advertising by pointing out that the food James is eating is not the traditional English fare he imagines it to be:

> In fact it's the invention of an advertising campaign they ran in the early sixties to encourage people to eat in pubs. A completely successful fabrication of the past, the Ploughman's Lunch was. (MA 106–7)

The phrase sums up not only the repressions and distortions of history on which Penfield and the nation are embarked, but the whole culture's infatuation with manufactured images.

The film delivers its indictment most obviously through the correspondences it forges between public and private, past and present, and through the crowning revelation that James is merely a pike amongst sharks; but some of its deadliest effects are achieved by mining the script with explosive details. For instance, while selling his idea for the Suez book over lunch, Penfield assures his wealthy publisher that he is not a socialist, but thirty scenes later, when he is buttering up Ann Barrington to worm his way into her daughter's affections, he answers the same question just as glibly in the affirmative. And in his keenness to mask his social origins from Susan, he kills off his doting parents with two brutal words: 'Both dead' (MA 57). His mother is indeed mortally ill, but after one perfunctory trip home to see her, he never finds time for her again. We eavesdrop twice as he meets his father's pleas over the phone with transparent lies about work making it impossible to visit. But it is the film's closing shot that delivers the coup de grâce:

> *A group of mourners round a grave. A grey day. A priest reads from the Book of Common Prayer, but his voice is virtually lost to us. We find James's father, hunched in his overcoat, face immobile with grief. Next to him, James, expressionless.*
>
> *James glances at his watch.*
>
> *Freeze frame. Optical zoom.* (MA 118)

To complain of the shortage of strong, upbeat characters who offer an alternative to Penfield and his ilk is to miss the point of *The Ploughman's Lunch*. McEwan cheerfully concedes that the central figures 'start out bad, and get worse' (MA 30). James survives being hoodwinked and uses his rage to write a successful book on Suez in record time. So we are denied the moral satisfaction of seeing this parasite's progress terminated and his ruthlessness punished. But as McEwan points out, 'moral values can be as easily, if not more plausibly, embodied in a narrative structure as in any right-thinking or suddenly reformed character' (MA 30). *The Ploughman's Lunch* shuns the mainstream cinema's addiction to positive identification, that 'nursery tale aesthetic' (MA 30) which doles out false hopes and sentimental consolations to passive consumers. McEwan had something else in mind: 'I wanted people both to be sucked in and to be left cold' (NI 187). The film works by absorbing its audience in a world which blocks their urge to identify at every turn and obliges them to adopt instead a detached, analytic standpoint, to put two and two together for themselves.

For McEwan the film's ultimate aim is to alert us to 'the uses we make of the past, and the dangers, to an individual as well as to a nation, of living without a sense of history' (MA 26). The point is made eloquently in the film by Ann Barrington when she remarks to James:

> The Czech writer Kundera has one of his characters say that the struggle of man against tyranny is the struggle of memory against forgetting . . . If we leave the remembering to historians then the

struggle is already lost. Everyone must have a memory, everyone needs to be a historian. (*MA* 76)

In this sense *The Ploughman's Lunch* is a militant act of historiography, which turns its viewers into vigilant adepts of Clio's art.

8

Back to the Future
The Child in Time

McEwan has given an illuminating account of the genesis of his third novel:

> In the summer of 1983, two months after *The Ploughman's Lunch* had been released, I found myself tilting my chair and daydreaming about a novel I might write. I began to make notes. I was about to become a father, and my thoughts were narrowed and intensified. I was haunted by the memory, or perhaps the memory of a dream, of a footpath that emerges onto a bend in a country road. It is luxuriant high summer, and there is a fine drizzle. There is a pub just along the road. A figure who is me and not me is walking towards it, certain that he is about to witness something of overwhelming importance. Writing *The Child in Time*, which took me to the end of 1986, was about the discovery of what that man saw. Other elements – a man pulled from the wreckage of a lorry, a birth, a lost child, a man who attempts to return to his childhood, an authoritarian childcare handbook, the elusive and protean nature of time – all these seemed to rotate about this central scene, and would somehow explain it, or contribute to it. (*MA* xxv–xxvi)

The new novel, which was to be his longest and most ambitious to date, would also incorporate what McEwan had learned from his libretto and his screenplay, bringing the visionary lyricism of the one into collision with the disenchanted realism of the other.

The Child in Time (1987) is set a decade into the future, in the middle of the nineties. The Britain of *The Ploughman's Lunch* has deteriorated even further after years of repressive government, drawing ominously closer to the Orwellian dystopia McEwan had sketched in 'Two Fragments: March 199-' in *In Between the Sheets*. As if 'the instinctive siding in all matters with the strong, the exaltation of self-interest, the selling-off of schools, the beggars, and so on' (p. 190) were not enough to contend with, mad weather feeds a creeping fear of ecological meltdown and the earth teeters permanently on the brink of nuclear Armageddon. Although proving prescient is the last thing on McEwan's mind, it would be hard to deny the epithet to his depiction of a Tory regime sharpening the nation's social and economic divisions, running down the welfare state, and disguising the rise of a police state ruled by the market as a return to law and order and traditional family values. In the midst of this desert of gloom, however, there blooms against all the odds an extravagant faith in the possibility of redemption through love and trust. *The Child in Time* has no political blueprint to pit against the future from which it recoils. But what it can offer is the inspiring tale of one man undergoing that 'evolutionary transformation of consciousness' (*MA* 15–16) so keenly foreseen in *Or Shall We Die?*

When the story begins, Stephen Lewis, a successful author of children's books, has lost both his daughter and his wife. Two years previously three-year-old Kate was stolen from under his nose at the supermarket and he has never seen her since. The tragedy has driven a wedge of guilty grief between Stephen and Julie, who has abandoned her husband to nurse her despair in the solitude of a remote cottage. Stranded alone in London, Stephen sinks into the mire of introspection so dear to McEwan's earliest protagonists, and seems doomed to fester indefinitely in this catatonic state. But on the day he visits Julie in her rural retreat after months of separation, he witnesses that 'something of overwhelming importance' which for McEwan was the germ of the novel – something wondrous which heralds the end of pain and the renewal of life and love. On the way to Julie's house Stephen stumbles upon a pub he knows he has never seen before, but which affects him with a sense, 'almost a kind of ache, of familiarity, of coming to a place that knew him too' (p. 56). He has slipped through a rift in the fabric of time itself, and for one awesome, mind-snapping moment he gazes through the window of The Bell into the eyes of his own mother, carrying his foetal self within her womb:

> He fell back down, dropped helplessly through a void, was swept dumbly through invisible curves and rose above the trees, saw the horizon below him even as he was hurled through sinuous tunnels of undergrowth, dark, muscular sluices. His eyes grew large and round and lidless with desperate, protesting innocence, his knees rose under

him and touched his chin, his fingers were scaly flippers, gills beat time, urgent, hopeless strokes through the salty ocean that engulfed the treetops and surged between their roots . . . (p. 60)

Stephen's mother subsequently corroborates his vertiginous epiphany and divulges its significance. That day the unborn Stephen's fate had hung in the balance, and it was the fancied sight of her grown-up son through the window that had decided her to let the child live. It is as if Stephen has been plucked from the future to ensure his own survival by intervening in the past.

Nor does the resonance of the incident die there. When Stephen reaches Julie's they make love, and for a brief interval not only are their old selves restored, but 'he did not doubt that what was happening now, and what would happen as a consequence of now, was not separate from what he had experienced earlier that day. Obscurely, he sensed a line of argument was being continued' (p. 63). At once the icy river of estrangement flows between them again, and Stephen resumes his reclusive routine. But Julie has conceived another child, whose unexpected birth at the close of the novel seals their reunion and begins to heal the gaping wound of their loss. The advent of the new child and the restoration of his wife make Stephen realize that his epiphany 'had not only been reciprocal with his parents', it had been a continuation, a kind of repetition', and 'that all the sorrow, all the empty waiting had been enclosed within meaningful time, within the richest unfolding conceivable' (p. 211). Earlier in the novel, Stephen had miraculously steered his way out of a crash and rescued a lorry-driver trapped upside-down inside the crushed cab of his vehicle. After peering 'into a dark chamber where the man's body could be seen curled' (p. 98), Stephen pulls the man out head-first through a 'vertical gash in the steel' (p. 96) in a scene which prefigures his delivery of his child at the end of the book. An event which had seemed random turns out to be a rehearsal, confirmation of that deeper patterning of time to which hindsight alone is privy.

The metamorphosis undergone by McEwan in the six years since his previous novel could scarcely seem more complete. *The Child in Time* introduces a novelist transfigured by his exposure to feminism, by political engagement and by paternity itself into a celebrant of loving parenthood and the marvel of maternity. Nothing signposts the distance McEwan has travelled more clearly than the history of Stephen's friend, the glamorous publisher and politician Charles Darke. Darke is consumed by the familiar McEwan fantasy of regression: 'He wanted the security of childhood, the powerlessness, the obedience, and also the freedom that goes with it, freedom from money, decisions, plans, demands' (pp. 200–1). So he abandons his meteoric career in mid flight and secludes himself in a rural sanctuary. Here he dresses and acts like an old-fashioned schoolboy, complete with catapult and pockets full of the marbles he has plainly lost. The futility of his yearning to dwell in this pathetic parody of a *Just William* world kills him, of course. He finally sits down in the freezing cold at the foot of his tree-house and gives up the ghost of his boyhood. Stephen is incredulous of his friend's imposture from the start, and when he carries his dead body home from the woods on his back, the scene serves as an image of McEwan himself bearing off the corpse of a cherished daydream he has long outgrown. It is as if the old male ego, that lonely doppelgänger with its dark obsessions, can at last be laid to rest by a self redeemed by fatherhood and true respect for the female body.

Yet in wedding his narrative so openly to a feminist vision McEwan inevitably attracts the charge of sacrificing imagination to ideology, exploration to opinion, and thus breaking his own golden rule for the novel. In *A Vain Conceit* (London, 1989) D. J. Taylor scolds 'McEwan's most obviously political book' (p. 58) for nailing its colours too firmly to the mast: 'Despite its continual felicities of style and observation, *The Child in Time* has still not solved the question of how far "politics" can go without irritating the reader or undermining the writer's sense of himself' (p. 59). The novel is indeed scarred by passages where McEwan does too much expounding and not enough implying, where the discursive scaffolding of the book has been incompletely dismantled. But the flaws of the novel are far outweighed by its accomplishments. It is telling a new kind of story about a new kind of experience, the liberation of men from masculinity, and it suffers from all the stumblings and embarrassments one might expect of such a pioneering venture. To subscribe to Adam Mars-Jones's dismissal of the novel in *Venus Envy* (London, 1990) as merely an extended couvade, which seeks 'to upstage or to appropriate potent moments in the lives of women' (p. 33), would be misguided. Mars-Jones has identified a thorny contradiction at the heart of *The*

Child in Time, but why he should have expected anything but contradiction from a male novelist's critique of the patriarchal mind is baffling.

Quite apart from the veiled urge to usurp female power, there is strong evidence that what Charles Darke embodies cannot be killed off so easily after all. For although Stephen's story culminates in mature paternity and marital bliss, it does so only by grace of an event which affords him the ultimate regressive satisfaction. In the paranormal episode at The Bell, mother and son communicate telepathically across time, need answering need in a moment of violent anachronism. But in the process Stephen trumps Darke's dream of relinquishing manhood by spiralling back still further to the cloistered innocence of the uterus. By reversing the forward flow of time and entropy a pristine embryonic state is restored, as the adult male reaches back to secure his own conception against the threat posed by his father's reluctance. The son returns to found his own existence, to anchor his own identity, by cutting out his biological father and, through an act of mystical communion with his mother, fathering himself.

Immediately after this act, indeed as a direct consequence of it, he proceeds to father his second child, the one that will repair his marriage and fill the void left by the stolen Kate. It is surely not fortuitous that the redemptive might of the new baby is premised on such a sinister vanishing. With any writer other than McEwan the traumatic abduction of a little girl and a guilt-stricken father might be glossed over as mere données. But with 'Butterflies' and 'In Between the Sheets' in mind, it is hard not to read into these premises the oblique indulgence of a less elevated craving – especially when the child's disappearance sweeps the mother from the scene as well, leaving her husband to hog the limelight.

The difference, of course, is that in this narrative the elimination of child and mother is a prelude to the sublime nativity which concludes the book and atones for their bloodless excision. The utopian finale is marred, nevertheless, by the envious couvade of which Mars-Jones complains, and for which the delivery of the lorry driver from his metal womb provides a heroic rehearsal. When Stephen rushes to the bedside of his pregnant wife, exactly nine months after the child's conception, he makes love to her once more and triggers her contractions. The long journey from ejaculation to parturition is telescoped into one short sequence which edits out the child's gestation within the mother. The scene arrogates control to the father, creating the illusion that the act of insemination instantly precipitates the birth. And because they are marooned in the country, the stage is set for Stephen to play the midwife and deliver his own child into the world.

The feminist romance of *The Child in Time* is inescapably tainted by obstinate dreams of erasing and supplanting women. But it would be a mistake to conclude from this that the novel is the sly haven of sexism and misogyny Mars-Jones claims to discern. It would be juster to see the book as locked in combat with its own assumptions and uncovering in the process a more complex truth than Mars-Jones's political correctness can accommodate. For *The Child in Time* does not pretend that a clean, uncompromised break with patriarchy is feasible. It recognizes that the desire to transfigure masculinity cannot be disentangled from the deep-rooted feelings it seeks to abolish. It knows that those unregenerate urges cannot simply be dismissed, that they will leave their coercive imprint on the new dispensation whether we like it or not.

The Child in Time is aware of the impossibility of leaping out of history into a purified space, uncontaminated by hierarchy, force, fear or envy. Nothing in the novel brings that realization home more movingly than the closing paragraphs, which capture unforgettably that instant on the threshold of history for which we all might be described as truly innocent:

> It was a beautiful child. Its eyes were open, looking towards the mountain of Julie's breast. Beyond the bed was the window through which they could see the moon sinking into a gap in the pines. Directly above the moon was a planet. It was Mars, Julie said. It was a reminder of a harsh world. For now, however, they were immune, it was before the beginning of time, and they lay watching planet and moon descend through a sky that was turning blue.
>
> They did not know how much later it was they heard the midwife's car stop outside the cottage. They heard the slam of its doors and the tick of hard shoes on the brick path.
>
> 'Well?' Julie said. 'A girl or a boy?' And it was in acknowledgement of the world they were about to rejoin, and into which they hoped to take their love, that she reached down under the covers and felt. (p. 220)

For one exquisite moment mother, child, and father are suspended in a kind of ecstasy, caught in a fleeting trance of unblemished hope and limitless possibility. Then the second hand of history moves on the face of time once more, a motion echoed in 'the tick of hard shoes on the brick path' as society invades the house in the guise of the midwife. The feminine moon declines and Mars, the symbol of the angry male world about to claim them, is once more in the ascendant. The imminent discovery of the baby's sex will confer on it the gender bound to shape its social destiny, turning it from a child outside time to the child in time, weaving it into the web of complicity human creatures seem unable to evade. No doubt McEwan leaves himself vulnerable to the charge of sentimentalism by exciting our nostalgia for that state of grace before the tide of history stole in and snatched us from the sandcastled beach. But maybe sentimentality is the minefield any attempt to touch the heart must cross.

9

Body Blow
The Innocent

Had any doubt remained about how tenaciously McEwan's earliest obsessions have continued to cling to his imagination, however much he may appear to have shaken them off, his fourth novel should have dispelled it. *The Innocent* (1990) is a cunning reprise of the recurrent motifs of McEwan's fiction: all the old haunts are revisited, the familiar fixations gathered up and woven together into a stylish tale of espionage and betrayal.

The Berlin setting in 1955 at the depth of the Cold War allows him to address again questions of history first posed in *The Imitation Game* and *The Ploughman's Lunch*. Writing on the eve of the Cold War's demise, as the Wall itself is about to collapse and forty years of nuclear fear begin to evaporate, McEwan turns back to explore the chilly dawn of the post-war epoch which shaped his own childhood and the polarized world in which he grew up. Telling that story involves chronicling another aspect of the end of the empire, the theme tackled so astutely in the Suez scenes of *The Ploughman's Lunch*. In this case the focus tightens on the eclipsing of Britain by the USA, both as a political and as a cultural force. It is not only a matter of recalling Britain's relegation to a cameo-role in the protracted show-down between East and West; equally significant is the nation's seduction by the American way of life, its greedy capitulation to an array of habits, tastes, and postures, whose absorption has turned once imperial Britain into an outpost of Uncle Sam's empire. The novel develops too the film's preoccupation with the way the psychology and morality of nations is mirrored in the psychology and morality of individuals. *The Innocent* shows how completely the innermost self can be penetrated and disfigured by desires cultivated in the public sphere.

Through its young hero, Leonard Marnham, the book turns once more to the male rites of passage that featured so strongly in McEwan's fiction during the seventies. Stranded far from his drab suburban home in the exciting, alien atmosphere of occupied Berlin, Marnham falls in love for the first time with an older woman named Maria Eckdorf, to whom he loses his virginity. Their heady romance culminates in another, less enchanting initiation in violence and death, when Marnham is forced to kill Maria's ex-husband Otto in self-defence and dispose of the corpse to conceal the deed. First love and last rites share yet another squeamish embrace, as McEwan reworks the necessary nightmare in which the body is acknowledged and annihilated, laid bare yet buried out of sight and mind. Marnham remains 'the scrubbed-clean innocent' (p. 81) in the shallow sense of not being to blame for the chain of events which leads him to butcher a man and (as he thinks) betray his country. But the novel's title acquires its pathos from a tragic sense of the end of innocence both for an individual and the country he stands for, as each stumbles into an era of lost simplicities.

The yearning to reclaim the magical immunity of boyhood or to retire even further into the fastness of the womb recurs in various forms in *The Innocent*. It crops up in its oedipal guise in Leonard's relationship with Maria, when the two withdraw into a secret erotic lair, a 'closed and clotted space' (p. 78) deep beneath the heaped blankets sheltering them from the freezing Berlin winter. Leonard's swift bewitchment by American habits is a surrender to a lifestyle designed to gratify infantile appetites. 'Much of the novel', as McEwan has pointed out, 'is concerned with Leonard overcoming his distaste for rock and roll and beginning to like freezing cold Coca Cola, and accepting that grown men might drink chocolate milk, accepting the paradox that this very powerful nation seems also to have a culture of the nursery' (*PP* 43). Above all there is Operation Gold itself, the surveillance tunnel being built under the East-West border by British and American intelligence to tap Russian communications. The novel has no illusions about what needs are really being fulfilled here:

> It was a toytown, packed with boyish invention. Leonard remembered the secret camps, the tunnels through the undergrowth he used to make with friends in a scrap of woodland near his house. . . Tunnels were stealth and safety; boys and trains crept through them, lost to sight and care, and then emerged unscathed. (pp. 71–2)

The path leading the innocent forward into adult knowledge and guilt loops ironically back through childish satisfactions. *The Innocent* also continues McEwan's engagement with the politics of gender. In Marnham it portrays a young man playing the imitation game, trying on and testing out styles of masculinity. Down in the tunnel he is inducted into a 'virile cult of competence' (p. 19) and the strict, unspoken codes of behaviour it enjoins on its members. Making love with Maria, vulnerable and uncertain before a more experienced woman, Leonard discovers 'the delicacy of masculine pride' (p. 58). The prospect of Otto's arriving to threaten their love provokes in him 'fantasies of confrontation' culled from film clichés: 'He saw himself in movie style, the peaceable tough guy, hard to provoke, but once unleashed, demonically violent' (p. 127). But in the fearful prelude to the actual fight with Otto, Maria goads him for his failure to meet the intrusion with rage and blows, 'accusing him of not being a man' (p. 146). Earlier, however, it had been his injection of brutality into their lovemaking, his attempt to act out the vicious rape scenarios that rise unbidden to his mind, that had almost destroyed their relationship: 'He had taken this woman and was forcing her. Half terrified, half in awe, she dared not disobey' (p. 84).

What excites him most, to his surprise and guilty pleasure, is 'the soldier fantasy' (p. 84) in which he casts Maria as a spoil of war, a woman of the defeated German nation whom he has the victor's right to ravish. As in *The Ploughman's Lunch*, we are invited to dwell on the reciprocity binding the conduct of a state to the private motivation of its subjects. But the episode echoes also the recognition in *The Comfort of Strangers* that more of our sexuality than most care to admit, including the pleasures of subjection, has been programmed into us so long ago that it lies beyond our conscious command:

> he started having thoughts that he was powerless to send away when he was making love. They soon grew inseparable from his desire. These fantasies came a little closer each time, and each time they continued to proliferate, to take new forms. There were figures gathering at the edge of thought, now they were striding towards the centre, towards him. They were all versions of himself, and he knew he could not resist them. (p. 83)

But it is not only Leonard's attempted violation of Maria that McEwan intends us to construe as a metaphor for the allied violation of Germany. The same idea is elaborated in the novel's most notorious scene: the stomach-turning account of the dismemberment of Otto's corpse on the table in Maria's apartment. McEwan has made clear what he had in mind when he wrote this scene: 'I'm interested in how a violent impulse grows inside us. In *The Innocent* a rather ordinary man is caught up in a difficult situation and becomes extremely violent. The protagonist's mind is full of images of the Second World War. I wanted to show the brutality man can aspire to by comparing the dismemberment of a corpse to the dismemberment of a city: the bomb-devastated Berlin of the post-war' (*PP* 41–2). Yet the mind does not linger long over the edifying gloss McEwan puts on the episode. The sheer protraction of the butchery and the sensuous absorption in gory surgical detail suggest that something tethered in the depths of his imagination has finally broken free.

In the early fiction the body had to be hidden – encased in concrete, swallowed by a river, or made invisible by the magic of solid geometry. But it was always forcing its way back from exile, smuggling itself in through smell or touch or sight. It left traces of itself in countless bodily secretions and emissions, in snot and sweat and sperm and spittle and blood. These glimpses of the moist internal texture of being betray the scandalous *secret de tous connu*, in whose preservation we all learn to conspire. What must be buried over and over again is our brute physicality, which explodes all pretence of transcendence by insisting that nothing but cultural illusions and accidents of evolution divide us from the most squalid life-forms. The title story of *First Love, Last Rites* glanced memorably at this knowledge in the image of the pregnant rat, whose ripped corpse divulged its biological kinship with its executioners. But in *The Innocent* the anaesthetic of displacement is withheld. We are obliged to gaze unblinking with McEwan at the visceral truth of human nature, whose mystery starts and ends right here in the obscenity Leonard Marnham lays bare.

As Leonard starts to saw through Otto's torso, we know as he knows that we are about to trespass into forbidden territory: 'He was in the cavity that contained all that he did not want to see' (pp. 180–1). When the half-severed trunk slips from his grasp, however, disgorging its contents onto the carpet, he has no choice but to see:

Before he made his run for the bathroom he had an impression of liverish reds, glistening irregular tubing of a boiled egg bluish white, and something purple and black, all of it shining and livid at the outrage of violated privacy, of secrets exposed. Despite the open windows, the room filled with the close stench of musty air, which itself was a medium for other smells: of sweet earth, sulphurous crap, and Sauerkraut. The insult was, Leonard had time to think as he stepped hurriedly round the up-ended halves of the torso that were still joined, that all this stuff was also in himself. (p. 182)

This is what the unfathomable complexity of human history and culture is spun out of and what it boils down to: the ultimate, crude secret on which the survival of our grander mysteries depends. The dead, dissected body is the point where signifying halts and hermeneutics ends, where the final ground of meaning is unmasked and metaphysical delusions implode. Hence the simultaneous horror and liberating gusto with which *The Innocent* assaults and defiles the human form.

A novel of espionage affords an apt medium in which to pursue this remorseless unfolding. There are many reasons why McEwan revisits the world of surveillance that first hooked him in *The Imitation Game*, but not the least important is the space it grants him to monitor his own procedures as a writer. Tunnelling down beneath the surface and burrowing across borders into forbidden territory to hijack and crack coded messages is a perfect image for what McEwan's fiction is up to. His imagination finds the universe mapped by Deighton and Le Carré so congenial because it gives both writer and reader the voyeuristic kick of invading privacy unseen and watching with impunity 'the slow unveiling of a secret' (p. 18). Like the spying game itself, *The Innocent* involves learning to unpack one layer of diversion after another to expose the ulterior motive. How close we actually get to this objective depends, in the jargon of the trade, on what level of clearance we acquire, which is something we can never know for sure. To quote Leonard's American boss, Bob Glass, whose mind is anything but as transparent as his surname suggests: 'everybody thinks his clearance is the highest there is, everyone thinks he has the final story. You only hear of a higher level at the moment you're being told about it' (p. 14). *The Innocent* lures us on from one level to the next by promising a terminal initiation, a final story, which will not turn out to be a stalking-horse for something else. But no sooner has it fulfilled its promise in Leonard's anatomy lesson than it breaks it by contesting that scene's sovereignty in the closing chapter.

The novel works admirably first of all as an engrossing spy thriller. Its persuasive factual feel is enhanced not only by McEwan's incorporation of Operation Gold, the extraordinary Berlin Tunnel actually built by the CIA and MI6, but by his including in the cast the notorious real-life double-agent, George Blake, who did indeed betray the project before it was even begun. And the elegant plot-line teases us with the mystery of how Leonard gets away with stowing the body in the tunnel, before solving it with the aid of Mr Blake in the penultimate paragraph. The spy yarn turns out to conceal a wry historical novel about the twilight of British supremacy, the triumph of American cultural imperialism and the ice age of the Cold War. Then the bottom slides out of this chronicle to reveal a *Bildungsroman*, in which a young man barters his guiltless heart for bittersweet carnal knowledge and a gruesome schooling in the craft of the abattoir. Squatting at the heart of this tale is the appalling spectacle of the demystified body, the black hole in the text through which meaning itself threatens to bleed away.

All that prevents it from doing so, all that staves off the dire conclusions spilling from Otto's abdomen, is the equally ultimate leap of faith made by the final chapter, which appends an auspicious postscript to the events of 1955–6. Thirty years on, in June 1987, Leonard Marnham returns to Berlin to visit the site of the tunnel and make his peace with the past. The novel closes with Leonard standing over the ruins of Operation Gold, only yards from the guarded Wall, reading the letter from Maria which holds out the prospect of reunion and forgiveness after all these years. The final sentence looks forward to a transfigured future in which mutual absolution and political deliverance converge: 'They would visit the old places and be amused by the changes, and yes, they would go out to Potsdamer Platz one day and climb the wooden platform and take a good long look at the Wall together, before it was all torn down' (p. 245).

10

Feeding the Void
Black Dogs

The Innocent ends on a sanguine note with its hero foreseeing the fall of the Berlin Wall and an end to the barbarities its existence sustained. In *Black Dogs* (1992) the narrator travels to Berlin with his father-in-law to join the jubilant crowds and witness the actual collapse of the Wall for himself. The Berlin air is charged with the expected feeling of festive release, but something else is brewing as well and it soon takes shape before them. At Checkpoint Charlie they become entangled in an ugly scene in which a young Turkish immigrant with a red flag is set upon by Neo-Nazi skinheads, while middle-class citizens in suits observe the assault with ill-disguised satisfaction. The incident confirms the vanity of any simple-minded, sentimental hopes the visitors might have harboured. As the monument to the defeat and division of Nazi Germany topples, a vicious new generation of racists emerges to take up the torch of fascism, and a terrible question takes shape: what if the event that seemed to mark the victory at last of reason and popular democracy turns out to hatch a basilisk?

This is the anxiety which lies behind the creation of *Black Dogs*. It is the widespread fear that, far from having left the apocalyptic horrors of both world wars behind, we may be en route to reliving them, because the human drives which fuelled them had merely been suppressed, and may never be eradicated. Developments not only in Germany but across eastern Europe since 1989 have shaken McEwan as much as anyone who shared his political vision, his trust in the possibility of social and sexual emancipation. *Black Dogs*, published only two years after *The Innocent*, substitutes for the latter's conclusion in rapprochement and renewal a closing prediction that the forces of darkness, symbolized by the ominous creatures of the title, 'will return to haunt us, somewhere in Europe, in another time' (p. 174). McEwan's mood in this novel is one of frank doubt and bewilderment, as the epigraph from the Renaissance humanist Marsilio Ficino attests: 'In these times I don't, in a manner of speaking, know what I want; perhaps I don't want what I know and want what I don't know.'

In *Black Dogs* McEwan stages the crisis into which his beliefs have been thrown and takes stock of what writing fiction entails. The novel compresses the diverse conflicts organizing his work to date into a single, searching debate. The contending viewpoints are embodied in the three principal figures between whom the narrative commutes: the narrator, Jeremy, and his wife's parents, Bernard and June Tremaine. Jeremy's Preface to his memoir of this couple, which furnishes the main substance of the novel, spells out the nature of the positions competing for the author's allegiance: 'Rationalist and mystic, commissar and yogi, joiner and abstainer, scientist and intuitionist, Bernard and June are the extremities, the twin poles along whose slippery axis my own unbelief slithers and never comes to rest' (p. 19). They also reincarnate the gendered distinction between the Newtonian and Einsteinian world-views in *Or Shall We Die?* and *The Child in Time*, and they hark back beyond that, of course, to the antagonism between Albert and Maisie in 'Solid Geometry'.

For Bernard, the rational scientific humanist who left the Communist Party after Hungary in 1956 and became a Labour MP, it is human beings who inscribe on reality whatever intelligibility it yields; we make things the way they are, and we can change them for better or worse by changing the way we think and behave as individuals and communities. For June, however, a momentous encounter with two gargantuan black dogs while on honeymoon in France in 1946 has been enough to convince her that a divinity shapes our ends, and that our lives should be devoted to cultivating its presence within us and resisting the incursions of its opposite, the pure malevolence manifest in the demonic hounds she fought off that day: 'I met evil and discovered God' (p. 60). From the standpoint of June, the author of *Ten Meditations* and *Mystical Grace: Selected Writings of St Teresa of Avila*, the soul is the battlefield on which a universal Manichaean war is perpetually waged, and the revolutionary politics to which she too had subscribed before her revelation are a fatal delusion, an evasion of the deeper truths of being and the more taxing obligations of the human heart.

June's vision strikes a chord with her son-in-law. With the incident at Checkpoint Charlie still fresh in his mind, he finds it hard to shake off her belief in an ineradicable taste for evil lurking in individuals and nations, an appetite 'no amount of social theory could account for' (p. 172). Fortunately, June maintains, to pit against this 'we have within us an infinite resource, a potential for a higher state of being, a goodness' and 'the healing power of love' (p. 60). But it is at this point that her biographer's sympathy departs in quest of Bernard's disabusing antidote, marshalling its aversion to 'those clarion calls to love, to improve, to yield up the defensible core of selfhood and see it dissolve in the warm milk of universal love and goodness. It is the kind of talk that makes me blush. I wince for those who speak this way. I don't see it, I don't believe it' (p. 60).

Yet the idealistic, future-bound politics of Bernard cannot detain Jeremy's credence much longer, as he beholds the spectre of fascism rising from the ruins of a wall erected in the name of socialism and the liberation of humanity. There is something arid and alienated about Bernard's masculine rationality – the detached, abstract gaze of the superior Cartesian self analysing and correcting the external world – which is plainly part of the problem. Jeremy recognizes in himself the same soulless contempt for the incalculable and distaste for the numinous, and finds himself pulled back into the gravitational field of Bernard's wife, wondering whether some malign or benign spiritual force might not be governing our destiny after all, making nonsense of our historical narratives and political designs.

As his mind shuttles back and forth between the two creeds, each strikes him by turns as banal, self-deceiving claptrap or urgent wisdom of global relevance, commanding unqualified assent. Listening to the two voices haranguing each other inside his head, he winds up paralysed, terminally stumped: 'Each proposition blocked the one before, or was blocked by the one that followed. It was a self-cancelling argument, a multiplication of zeros, and I could not make it stop' (pp. 119–20). Like Bernard and June themselves, who have lived apart, despite loving each other, for most of their married lives, the stances wrangling inside the narrator's skull are doomed to remain wedded yet unreconciled. So where does that leave the author? Jeremy should not be naïvely equated with Ian McEwan, but it would be equally naïve not to recognize how much of the novelist is mirrored in his creation. McEwan is writing a family history of his own adopted ideas, turning the searchlight on himself to find out what he has come to think and what kind of author writing has made him. The self-portrait is varnished with self-mocking irony. Jeremy describes himself as running 'a small publishing company specialising in text books' (p. 74). His own biography reads like a résumé of McEwan's fixations. Jeremy is an orphan, who lost his parents in a road accident at the age of eight and became obsessed with appropriating other people's parents, until his marriage supplied Bernard and June, and then fatherhood stilled the ache by turning him into a parent himself. His whole life has been a quest to compensate for the demise of childhood and the loss of mother and father by recreating that triangular liaison in another guise, by resurrecting infancy and so assuaging his 'irreducible sense of childish unbelonging' (p. 17). Experience has taught him 'that the simplest way of restoring a lost parent was to become one yourself; that to succour the abandoned child within, there was no better way than having children of your own to love' (p. 18). Jeremy's compassion for that forsaken inner child finds outward expression in his youthful love for his niece Sally, the battered baby of his reckless sister Jean, and in his gallant defence years later of a little boy tormented by his parents in a French hotel.

But alongside, perhaps inseparable from, this empathy with the vulnerable is what Jeremy himself calls 'my predatory nature': the writer's compulsion to give himself life by feeding off the life of others, to fill the vacuum in himself by draining meaning from the souls of his fellow creatures. *Black Dogs* is, amongst many other things, a study of the writer at work, a sinister portrait of the artist as vampire. Jeremy stalks his surrogate parents with a ravenous, intrusive absorption, following their spoor back to their first meeting and first time in bed, and tracking June's story through her last months in a nursing home and into the graveyard at her funeral. It is as if, by reviving their younger selves and reliving the origin of their estrangement, he is able to animate himself, to acquire an identity and solidity he would otherwise lack. 'A balding man of severe expression' (p. 49), 'the family outsider' (p. 50) in whom June identifies the same infuriating 'dryness and distance' (p. 53) that attracted her to Bernard, Jeremy sits by the bed of his dying 'adopted mother' (p. 31), notebook in hand, and becomes the go-between through whom the two continue their feud: 'I felt myself to be weightless, empty-headed, suspended in my uncertainty between two points' (p. 59).

Throughout his conversations with both his surrogate parents over several years Jeremy makes a troubling discovery:

> I discovered that the emotional void, the feeling of belonging nowhere and to no one that had afflicted me between the ages of eight and thirty-seven had an important intellectual consequence: I had no attachments, I believed in nothing. It was not that I was a doubter, or that I had armed myself with the useful scepticism of a rational curiosity, or that I saw all arguments from all sides; there was simply no good cause, no enduring principle, no fundamental idea which I could identify, no transcendent entity whose existence I could truthfully, passionately or quietly assert. (p. 18)

The state of negative capability, the writer's sponge-like gift for soaking up all kinds of conflicting selves and standpoints, can also be viewed as that 'emotional void', which relentlessly sucks other selves into its maw to replenish its energies. This consideration puts an intriguing spin on the significance of McEwan's black dogs.

The narrator gives the last word, and thus much weight, to June's belief that these creatures embody 'A malign principle, a force in human affairs that periodically advances to dominate and destroy the lives of individuals or nations, then retreats to await the next occasion' (p. 19). But Bernard's less portentous conclusion is called to witness too: 'Face to face with evil? I'll tell you what she was up against that day – a good lunch and a spot of village gossip!' (p. 173). The rumour that these beasts had once been Gestapo guard dogs used to rape French women as well as track down the Maquis is dismissed by him as melodramatic fantasy. In his Preface Jeremy enters the first of many caveats about investing the hounds with a significance they cannot bear: 'Whether June's black dogs should be regarded as a potent symbol, a handy catch phrase, evidence of her credulity or a manifestation of a power that really exists, I cannot say' (p. 19). Beguiling as they are, scepticism must remain the watchword: 'Turning-points are the inventions of storytellers and dramatists, a necessary mechanism when a life is reduced to, traduced by, a plot, when a morality must be distilled from a sequence of actions, when an audience must be sent home with something unforgettable to mark a character's growth' (p. 50). And as such they are deeply suspicious contrivances: 'these almost non-existent animals were too comforting' (p. 50).

If the black brutes that poisoned June's honeymoon and sabotaged her marriage were indeed Gestapo dogs and hence the quintessence of fascist barbarity, they would at least make sense as an expression of evil, whether social, natural or supernatural in provenance. But what if the creatures defy comprehension and judgement? The moment the young June perceives the snarling hounds about to devour her as evil incarnate, a complementary confidence in the might of pure goodness springs up within her: the terror is named and housed in a moral framework which allows her to cope. In fact the place in which McEwan sets this scene is far more frightening than the animals he lets loose in it to savage June. It is a steep, bleak, godforsaken gorge carved out of an equally desolate limestone landscape, whose sheer emptiness and 'ageless silence' (p. 139) engulf her. She feels helpless before the pitiless indifference of the harsh, precipitous cliffs. The sight of plant life clinging blindly to 'a vertical wall of baking rock' beheld 'across half a mile of bright, empty space' only intensifies her 'deep nausea' and apprehension of 'a darkness just beyond the reach of vision' (p. 141). The landscape refuses to be humanized and sentimentalized; it tears away every consoling anthropocentric illusion, disdaining domestication as picturesque or sublime: 'this place was their enemy' (p. 142). It is out of this ambience that the infernal curs materialize.

What the encounter with the dogs actually reveals is the affinity of man and beast in 'the bitter cause of survival' (p. 142) on the face of a careless planet. 'Out here the rules were exposed as mere convention, a flimsy social contract. Here, no institutions asserted human ascendancy. There was only the path which belonged to any creature that could walk it' (p. 147). The real revelation is staring at June from her predator's jaw:

> the alien black gums, slack black lips rimmed by salt, a thread of saliva breaking, the fissures on a tongue that ran to smoothness along its curling edge, a yellow-red eye, and eye-ball muck spiking the fur, open

sores on a fore leg, and trapped in the V of an open mouth, deep in the hinge of the jaw, a little foam to which her gaze kept returning. (p. 148)

The image has the same abrupt authority as the burst rat's belly in 'First Love, Last Rites' and the secrets slithering from Otto's abdomen in *The Innocent*. It inflicts the cruel knowledge that life is things devouring each other, literally or figuratively, and to no end other than the blind reproduction of that process. Seeing the dogs as satanic is a blessing by comparison, since it leaves our centrality and dignity as humans intact. No wonder June grabs that rationalization with such alacrity.

But a remorseless biological perspective is intolerable, as Leonard Marnham learns in *The Innocent* after disembowelling Otto: 'The thought of taking selected parts of the solid world and passing them through a hole in his head and squeezing them through his guts was an abomination' (*The Innocent*, 185). To sustain the dispassionate gaze of the zoologist, seeing humans as no more than 'newfangled apes' (p. 116) on a continuum with reptiles and scorpions is impossible for the humanist imagination. The recognition that we are the dupes of a physiology bereft of ulterior import must be screened off behind thickets of diverting fictions, designed to defer the return of that knowledge. This may be the true art of narrative: to spin pattern and transcendence out of the blank indifference of biology, to disguise the nature of life from itself.

Not the least disturbing disclosure of *Black Dogs* is that the narrator embodies the vision he strives to conceal. The emptiness of the fatal gorge where the beasts emerge mirrors the self-confessed void, the emotional and moral vacuum, within Jeremy himself. In the dogs' implacable jaws the writer finds figured his own rapacity and rootless blankness. The black dogs are an image of the insatiable vortex at the core of the creative imagination, the greedy source of narrative itself, and in these demonic creatures the author salutes his own kind. They mark the nagging lack of meaning in the real and in the writer which narration soothes with illusions of plenitude.

In his Preface Jeremy makes a brave stab at stating an ultimate creed which escapes the clutch of what the black dogs intimate. 'I would be false to my own experience,' he writes, 'if I did not declare my belief in the possibility of love transforming and redeeming a life' (p. 20). But unlike the leap of faith with which

The Innocent concludes, this solitary affirmation cannot offset the insight depressing the other side of the scales. In *Black Dogs* McEwan squares up to the fact that nothing can fill the abyss into which his novel peers. All we have is the fleeting respite of the stories we tell ourselves, the fictions we concoct to feed our hunger for sense. McEwan's omnivorous art of unease prowls on.

Select Bibliography

WORKS BY IAN McEWAN

First Love, Last Rites (London: Jonathan Cape, 1975; Pan Books/Picador, 1976). Short stories.

In Between the Sheets (London: Jonathan Cape, 1978; Pan Books/Picador, 1979). Short stories.

The Cement Garden (London: Jonathan Cape, 1978; Pan Books/Picador, 1980).

The Imitation Game: Three Plays for Television (London: Jonathan Cape, 1981; Pan Books/Picador, 1982).

The Comfort of Strangers (London: Jonathan Cape, 1981; Pan Books/Picador, 1982).

Or Shall We Die? Words for an Oratorio Set to Music by Michael Berkeley (London: Jonathan Cape, 1983).

The Ploughman's Lunch (London: Methuen, 1985). Screenplay.

Roberto Innocenti, *Rose Blanche*, text by Ian McEwan based on a story by Christophe Gallaz (London: Jonathan Cape, 1985). Picture book for children.

The Child in Time (London: Jonathan Cape, 1987; Pan Books/Picador, 1988).

Soursweet (London: Faber and Faber, 1988). Screenplay based on Timothy Mo's novel *Sour Sweet* (1982).

A Move Abroad: Or Shall We Die? and The Ploughman's Lunch (London: Pan Books/Picador, 1989).

The Innocent (London: Jonathan Cape, 1990; Pan Books/Picador, 1990).

Black Dogs (London: Jonathan Cape, 1992; Pan Books/Picador, 1993).

Uncollected Short Stories
'Intersection', in *Tri-Quarterly*, Fall 1975, 63–86.
'Untitled', in *Tri-Quarterly*, Winter 1976, 62–3.

'Deep Sleep, Light Sleeper', in *Harpers and Queen*, August 1977, 82–5.

INTERVIEWS

Casademont, Rosa González, 'The Pleasure of Prose Writing vs Pornographic Violence: An Interview with Ian McEwan', *The European English Messenger*, vol. 1, no. 3 (Autumn 1992), 40–5. Topics covered include McEwan's debt to Kafka, the origins of *The Innocent*, politics and the novel.

Haffenden, John, *Novelists in Interview* (London: Methuen, 1985), 168–90. Essential reading: deals in depth with all the major writings from *First Love, Last Rites* to *The Ploughman's Lunch*.

Hamilton, Ian, 'Points of Departure', *New Review*, vol. 5, no. 2 (Autumn 1978), 9–21. Invaluable source of biographical information about McEwan's childhood, schooling and first stabs at writing. Discusses short stories and *The Cement Garden*.

Ricks, Christopher, 'Adolescence and After' *Listener* (12 April 1979), 526–7. Contains illuminating reflections on *The Cement Garden*, 'Psychopolis', 'Homemade', 'To and Fro', as well as broader questions of vision and intent.

On Video

Writers Talk: Ideas of Our Time, Guardian Conversations, no. 69, Institute of Contemporary Arts. Ian McEwan in conversation with Martin Amis: absorbing exchange, chiefly concerned with *The Child in Time*, from which McEwan gives a reading.

BIOGRAPHICAL AND CRITICAL STUDIES

Banks, J. R., 'A Gondola Named Desire', *Critical Quarterly*, vol. 24, no. 2 (Summer 1982), 27–31. On *The Comfort of Strangers*, tracing its sexual themes back through the stories, *The Cement Garden* and *The Imitation Game*.

Elsässer, Thomas, 'The Ploughman's Lunch', *Monthly Film Bulletin*, vol. 50, no. 593 (June 1983), 165. A harsh critique of the film for its alleged 'glib nihilism' and lack of complexity.

Fletcher, John, 'Ian McEwan', *Dictionary of Literary Biography 14: British Novelists Since 1960, Part 2: H–Z* (Detroit: Gale, 1983), 495–500. Charts McEwan's career from beginnings at the University of East Anglia to *The Comfort of Strangers*, highlighting the neglected black humour of his work.

Grant, Damian and McEwan, Ian, *Contemporary Writers: Ian McEwan*, pamphlet co-published by the Book Trust and the British Council (London, 1989). Includes a brief but suggestive essay by Grant and an instructive statement by McEwan about the 'contradictory fantasies and aspirations' that rule his writing.

Lewis, Peter, 'McEwan, Ian (Russell)', *Contemporary Novelists*, ed. Lesley Henderson, 5th edn. (Chicago and London: St James Press, 1991), 621–3. Reviews the principal fiction up to *The Innocent*, arguing that a strong moral vision underlies McEwan's 'nihilism, morbidity and gothicism'.

Marecki, Joan E., 'McEwan, Ian (Russell) 1948–', *Contemporary Authors: New Revision Series* (Detroit: Gale, 1985), vol. 14, 312–13. A useful compilation of reviewers' responses to the stories and the first two novels.

Mars-Jones, Adam, *Venus Envy*, Chatto Counterblasts no. 14 (London: Chatto and Windus, 1990). A joint assault on Martin Amis and McEwan, indicting the latter for hijacking feminism in *The Child in Time*.

Massie, Allan, *The Novel Today: A Critical Guide to the British Novel 1970–1989* (London: Longman, 1990), pp. 49–52. Finds the early fiction marred by an 'immature' reliance on shock and fantasy, from which *The Child in Time* breaks free.

McEwan, Ian, 'An Only Childhood: Ian McEwan Remembers Growing Up Without Brothers and Sisters', *Observer*, 31 January 1982, p. 41. Offers fascinating insights into the sources of McEwan's obsession with guilt, innocence and the end of childhood.

Moriarty, Michael, 'A Pint of Barthes and a Ploughman's Lunch', *LTP: Journal of Literature Teaching Politics*, no. 3 (1984), 79–90. Intriguing political analysis of the film, using ideas drawn from Roland Barthes 'to examine the relations between ideology and the pleasure of the text'.

Ricks, Christopher, 'Playing with Terror', *London Review of Books*, vol. 4, no. 1 (21 January – 3 February 1982), 13–14. Perceptive account of *The Comfort of Strangers*; especially good on its debt to Ruskin on Venice and cunning deployment of names.

Sampson, David, 'McEwan/Barthes', *Southern Review* (Adelaide), vol. 17, no 1 (March 1984), 68–80. Elaborate poststructuralist interpretation of *The Cement Garden* as a text which subverts conventional modes of reading.

Taylor, D. J., 'Ian McEwan: Standing Up for the Sisters', in *A Vain Conceit: British Fiction in the 1980s* (London: Bloomsbury, 1989), pp. 55–9. Takes McEwan to task for allowing his political and feminist sympathies to compromise the quality of his fiction, most notably *The Child in Time*.

Index